Stock Options

An Authoritative Guide to Incentive and Nonqualified Stock Options

Robert R. Pastore, C.P.A.,
Chartered Financial Analyst

PCM Capital Publishing
1001 Bridgeway, #113
Sausalito, California 94965

For information on how to order *Stock Options: An Authoritative Guide to Incentive and Nonqualified Stock Options* contact PCM Capital Publishing, 1001 Bridgeway, #113, Sausalito, California 94965, or via E-mail at rpastore@usa.net.

© Robert R. Pastore, 1998
First Printing 1999

International Standard Book Number 0-9668899-1-6
Library of Congress Catalog Card Number 98-94198

Printed in the United States of America

Acknowledgements

Several friends contributed to the success of this project.

First and foremost, I am extremely grateful to Mike Griesmer, a partner in the public accounting firm *McClintock Accountancy Corporation* in Truckee, California. His insightful comments and business acumen helped to make this book unique. Mike is a brilliant tax professional, a man of integrity, and a loyal friend.

Ariel Abramsky, with her command of the English language, stressed the importance of writing succinctly. I will be forever thankful for the suggestions that she, Lane Brennan and Bruce Dunlap made for the jacket.

Kate Dumont brought clarity and concise expression through her copy editing.

My sincere thanks to Nelson Furlano, CPA. For years, he has offered me sound business advice and a helping hand.

Jaci Groves did library research – always willingly and always with a smile.

Over the years, I've known John McIvor to make wise choices. My thanks to him for the suggestions on jacket design.

My thanks to Angelo Menconi. He took the photograph that appears on the jacket.

Linda Mitchell, enjoyable to work with and very accommodating, created a beautiful cover design.

My uncle, Frederick "Pete" Wilkinson read the manuscript, one word at a time. He is responsible for making the final product user friendly.

My special thanks to many friends that offered words of encouragement.

I edited the manuscript at the *Sausalito Bakery & Café*. With their usual hospitality, Mahin, Kamelia, Iraj, Kambiz and Homayoon greeted me with warm smiles, a glass of water, and an espresso. My thanks to these wonderful friends and the nice people who frequent their café.

Finally, a special thanks to my parents, Agnese (Inez) and Vittorio Pastore, for stressing the importance of education.

Contents

6

IRS FORM 1040 REPORTING   87

Appendix - Tax Research   95

"She" and "He"

This book was written for both female and male optionees. With all due respect to you, the narrative uses the pronoun "he" while examples contain the pronoun "she".

Warning – Disclaimer

This book was written to provide general guidance to a large audience. Yet, every person who reads *Stock Options: An Authoritative Guide to Incentive and Nonqualified Stock Options* has unique needs and circumstances – including a unique income tax position. If legal, accounting or other expert services are required, a competent professional should be contacted.

Stock Options is a supplement to information contained in published articles and other texts, not as a complete guide to compensatory stock options. You are urged to read as much other material as you can on this subject.

While every effort has been made to make this book error-free, it may contain mistakes, both typographical and in content. In addition, the text is based on tax law and regulations in effect at the time the book was printed. The author and PCM Capital Publishing shall not be liable nor responsible to anyone for any loss or damage caused, or alleged to be caused, either indirectly or directly, from the information contained herein.

If you are unwilling to be bound by this disclaimer, you may return the book within seven days after the date of purchase and your purchase price will be refunded.

1

Introduction

Management realizes that competent **PEOPLE** are crucial to the corporation's success. They often retain such people by granting them options to purchase the company's stock.

Unfortunately, while the *intention* of management and the board of directors is to motivate and reward people through stock options, the *reality* is that much of the potential wealth that *could* come from those options is *wasted*. Why?

The answer is simple. Options are complicated. *If* people maximize the value of their options, it's usually by luck...*blind luck*.

Stock Options: An Authoritative Guide to Incentive and Nonqualified Stock Options was written as an educational tool to keep wealth in the hands of optionees who have earned it through hard work and dedication.

COMPENSATORY STOCK OPTIONS

Corporations often grant stock options to employees and non-employees (optionees) as a form of compensation. Consequently, such grants are commonly referred to as *compensatory* stock options. For purposes of federal income and employment taxation, compensatory stock options are classified as either *incentive stock options* (ISOs) or *nonqualified stock options* (NQSOs).

INCENTIVE STOCK OPTION

The incentive stock option (ISO), granted only to *employees*, describes an option that has satisfied the qualification requirements under Internal Revenue Code Section 422(b).

An ISO gives the optionee the right, but not the obligation, to purchase the stock of his employer or its parent or subsidiary corporation, at a fixed price (the *exercise price*), for a period of time not to exceed 10 years from the date the option is granted. The term of the option may not exceed *five* years for an individual that owns stock possessing more than 10 percent of the total combined voting power of all classes of stock of the employer corporation or of its parent or subsidiary corporation.

The optionee may exercise the ISO only during the time that he is an employee of the corporation that has granted the option, or a related corporation of such corporation, or within three months (12 months for an employee who satisfies the Internal Revenue Code's definition of "disabled") after termination of such employment.

NONQUALIFIED STOCK OPTION

A nonqualified stock option (NQSO) is a compensatory option that does *not* meet the qualification requirements of an incentive stock option. Nonqualified stock options may be granted to both employees, *and* non-employees (for example, directors and outside consultants).

RELEVANT ISSUES FOR OPTIONEES

Portfolio management, income taxation, and the cash requirements necessary to exercise options are three important issues facing optionees.

PORTFOLIO MANAGEMENT

Over time, the unrealized appreciation in compensatory stock options may be large relative to the optionee's total net worth.

That net worth could decline substantially if the price of the optioned stock declines. In short, the optionee's portfolio is not well diversified.

It is risky to hold a poorly diversified investment portfolio. That risk is compounded when the expected returns from the optionee's investments are highly correlated with the future cash flows that he expects to generate from his labor.

Example: Linda is an employee of ABC Corporation (ABC). A large portion of her net worth consists of unrealized appreciation in ABC stock options.

If the price of ABC stock declines substantially, a large portion of Linda's net worth evaporates. Linda is also dependent upon ABC for her semimonthly paycheck.

If Linda *isn't* uncomfortable in this position, she probably *should* be. Faced with a similar situation, some optionees wisely decide to exercise options, both incentive stock options and nonqualified stock options, and *immediately* sell the stock - triggering the recognition of taxable compensation income. They reinvest the after-tax proceeds from the sale of stock in other assets – stocks, fixed-income securities, real estate, cash equivalents, etc. - as appropriate, given their unique needs and circumstances.

INCOME TAXATION

Ordinary Income versus Long-term Capital Gain

In recent years, Congress substantially reduced the maximum income tax rate on long-term capital gain. The *maximum* rate of tax on gain from stock held for more than 12 months is now 20 percent. That 20 percent rate is almost 50 percent *less* than the 39.6 percent maximum tax rate on ordinary income.

Naturally, then, individuals are anxious – sometimes *too* anxious - to convert what would otherwise be taxed as ordinary income into more favorably-taxed, long-term capital gain. In fact, a large number of optionees that hold ISOs will be surprised to learn that for them, paying *more* income tax *now*, rather than *less* income tax *later*, is a wealth-*maximizing* strategy.

Other Important Tax Issues

The income tax consequences vary for stock options. Transactions that involve incentive stock options are taxed differently from those that involve nonqualified stock options.

Some of the more common tax considerations affecting optionees include:

- Exercising ISOs and selling the stock on the same day versus exercising ISOs and selling the stock 12 months and one day later

- Disqualifying versus non-disqualifying dispositions of stock

- Alternative minimum tax (AMT) issues relating to ISOs

- The *basis* of stock acquired by ISO exercise may be different for regular tax purposes than for AMT

- Tax withholding

- Restrictions imposed by U.S. securities law on sales of stock and the income tax implications of such restrictions

- Early exercise of NQSOs

- The IRC Section 83(b) election

CASH REQUIREMENTS

By its very terms, an option requires the optionee to pay the exercise price in order to buy the stock. This requirement is an important issue, and a common problem, for optionees who don't have the cash necessary to exercise their options.

To solve that problem, publicly-traded companies usually make arrangements with a brokerage firm. Such arrangements allow optionees to finance an option exercise with a same-day sale of stock, in a *cashless exercise*.

Under the terms of a cashless exercise, the optionee does *not* pay cash to exercise the option. The option is exercised (in other words, the optionee purchases the stock at the exercise price) and the brokerage firm sells the stock. Both the option exercise and the sale of stock occur on the same day. The optionee receives the excess of the proceeds from the sale of stock over the exercise price, on *settlement date* – without advancing any money to execute the transaction.

Every one of these important issues – portfolio management, income taxation, and cash requirements - is discussed extensively in the chapters that follow. These discussions will help to ensure that optionees have a more comprehensive understanding of the income tax and cash flow effects of impending transactions that involve compensatory stock options. With this knowledge, they are far less likely to rely on blind luck when it comes to maximizing the value of their options.

WHEN TO EXERCISE OPTIONS

The *general rule* is that an optionee should *not* be anxious to exercise compensatory stock options. Generally, he should *not* exercise them years before their expiration date.

The reasoning is simple and logical. First, compensatory stock options are somewhat similar to *interest-free loans* – loans that bear no interest. An interest-free loan has value (to the borrower) and the longer the amount of time remaining until the loan's maturity date, the more valuable it is (to the borrower), other things being equal.

Second, holding options *defers the payment of income taxes* on the taxable income that *would* be triggered by an option exercise.

EXCEPTIONS TO THE GENERAL RULE

There are many exceptions to the general rule that compensatory options should not be exercised well in advance of their expiration date.

Circumstances that may favor early exercise include:

- the optionee's need for cash

- the desire to diversify his investment portfolio

- a gradual process of exercising options, and selling the stock, as part of a longer-term strategy to minimize the impact of income taxation

- the fact that he has large capital loss carryovers that may not be useable in the near future because of the annual limitation on the income tax deductibility of capital losses. Such capital loss carryovers can be used to offset capital gains from the eventual sale of stock previously acquired by exercise of ISOs or NQSOs

- exercising NQSOs, or exercising ISOs and selling the stock in a disqualifying disposition, to accelerate income into a year in which he has *excess* income tax deductions that will otherwise expire (this strategy effectively results in *tax-free* income)

- exercising NQSOs and holding the stock in order to convert appreciation in the stock price after the date of option exercise from ordinary income into capital gain (long-term, or short-term, depending on whether or not he holds the stock for more than 12 months after exercise date)

Under certain circumstances, an optionee might find it attractive to exercise an option to purchase stock, even though the fair market value of the stock on the date of exercise is less than the option exercise price. It is far more likely, however, that optionees exercise options only when the fair market value of the stock on the date of exercise is equal to or greater than the option exercise price. *Consequently, all references in this text assume that on the date of option exercise, the fair market value of the stock equals or exceeds the option exercise price.*

2

Nonqualified Stock Options

Chapter 2 explains the *federal* income tax consequences regarding transactions that involve nonqualified stock options. Although *state* income tax law often works in tandem with federal law, often is different from always.

The optionee generally does *not* recognize taxable income on the date that a corporation grants him a nonqualified stock option. Instead, he generally recognizes ordinary compensation income on the date that he *exercises* the option.

On the date that he *does* recognize taxable income, such income is subject to federal income tax withholding, social security tax withholding, and medicare tax withholding - *whether or not he sells the stock.* These withholding taxes can be an unpleasant surprise to unsuspecting optionees – especially those who are under the (false) impression that withholding taxes are not required until the stock is sold.

While he *generally* recognizes taxable income on the date of option *exercise*, the executive that is prohibited by U.S. securities law from selling stock at the time of option exercise does *not* recognize taxable income on the date of option exercise. He recognizes income on the date that the restriction *ends* – unless he makes a timely tax election to recognize the income on the date of exercise. When and how to file such an election is an important part of this chapter.

IMPORTANT DATES

GRANT DATE

In most cases, the optionee does *not* recognize taxable income on the date of grant. This income tax treatment may arise because the terms of the option have been cleverly drafted to escape income taxation on the grant date.

More likely, however, the optionee does not recognize income on the date of grant because the option does not have a *readily ascertainable fair market value* (for example, the option is not publicly traded) on the date of option grant. The option does not have an ascertainable fair market value, for example, even though *standardized* option contracts on the company's stock may be publicly traded on the Chicago Board Options Exchange (CBOE). This is the case, for example, because the terms of the NQSO are different from the terms of the standardized option contract.

If the option does not have a readily ascertainable fair market value, Section 83 of the Internal Revenue Code (IRC) and U.S. Treasury Regulation 1.83-7 provide that the optionee does *not* recognize taxable income on the date of grant.

EXERCISE DATE

For the reasons discussed above, the optionee generally recognizes ordinary compensation income on the date that he *exercises* the option – *not* on the date of grant. The *amount* of income that he recognizes is equal to the excess of the fair market value of the stock on the date of option exercise over the exercise price.

INCOME TAX WITHHOLDING AND EMPLOYMENT TAXATION

Gain from the *exercise* of a nonqualified stock option is subject to income tax withholding, in addition to social security and medicare tax withholding on the date of exercise.

Withholding on the amount of ordinary compensation income that the optionee recognizes is required *even if the optionee does not sell the stock.* Consequently, those who intend to exercise NQSOs, and *hold* the stock, must be prepared to pay *not only* the exercise price to effect the stock purchase, but also the required withholding taxes.

BASIS OF STOCK ACQUIRED

The optionee's *basis* in the stock acquired by exercise of a nonqualified stock option is equal to the *fair market value* of the stock on the date of option exercise. It consists of two components - the amount of the exercise price *plus* the amount of ordinary compensation income that the optionee recognizes on the date of exercise.

Basis becomes an important issue on the date that the stock is sold. Capital gain or loss on the sale of stock acquired by exercise of NQSOs, as well as ISOs, is equal to the difference between the proceeds from the sale and the basis of the stock that is sold.

SALE DATE

On the date of sale, the optionee recognizes a *capital gain or loss* in the amount of the difference between the proceeds from the sale and the fair market value (basis) of the stock on the date of option exercise.

If the date of sale is more than 12 months after the date of option exercise, the gain or loss is taxed as long-term capital gain or loss. If the sale date is not more than 12 months after the date of option exercise, the gain or loss is taxed as short-term capital gain or loss.

BLACKOUT PERIODS

At times, securities law prohibits the optionee from selling stock in what is sometimes referred to as a *blackout period.* This restriction *alters* the federal tax consequences that normally occur on the date of option exercise.

As discussed earlier, the optionee generally recognizes ordinary compensation income on the date that he *exercises* the option. The amount of income that he recognizes is equal to the excess of the fair market value of the stock at the time of option exercise over the exercise price. This tax treatment *does not apply* when securities law prohibits the optionee from selling the stock at the time of option exercise.

Instead, the optionee recognizes ordinary compensation income on the date that the restriction *ends*, in the amount of the excess of the fair market value of the stock over the option's exercise price on the date that the restriction *ends* - unless the optionee makes a *timely* election under IRC Section 83(b) to recognize taxable income on the date of exercise.

In other words, if securities law prohibits the optionee from selling the shares acquired by option exercise, tax law offers him a choice - a choice that holders of NQSOs don't otherwise have. He may *choose* to recognize income on the date of *exercise* (as opposed to the date on which the restriction ends) in the amount of the excess of the fair market value of the stock on the date of *exercise* over the exercise price (as opposed to the excess of the fair market value over the exercise price on the date the restriction ends). He does this by filing an *election* under Internal Revenue Code Section 83(b) not later than 30 days after the date of option exercise.

Example: Lauren is an officer of XYZ Corporation, a publicly-traded company. On December 27, Year 1 Lauren exercises a NQSO on one share of XYZ stock at an exercise price of $70 per share. The fair market value of the stock on the date of exercise is $100 per share. The fair market value of the stock on January 16, Year 2 is $120.

On the date of exercise, and continuing through January 15, Year 2, securities law prohibits Lauren from selling stock of XYZ Corporation. If she does *not* make a timely election under IRC Section 83(b) to recognize $30 ($100 - 70) of ordinary compensation income on December 27, Year 1, U.S. Treasury Regulation 1.83-(3)(j) provides that Lauren recognizes *$50* of ordinary compensation income ($120 - 70) on January 16, Year 2, the date on which the blackout period ends.

U.S. Treasury Regulation 1.83-2 explains when, where and how to make a valid election under IRC Section 83(b).

IRC SECTION 83(b) ELECTION

As discussed earlier, optionees who are subject to blackout periods that prohibit them from selling stock acquired by exercise of a nonqualified stock option may find it prudent to recognize taxable income *early*. They do this by filing an election under Internal Revenue Code Section 83(b).

WHEN TO MAKE THE ELECTION

The election, *irrevocable* unless the optionee receives consent from the Internal Revenue Service (IRS), must be filed not later than 30 days after the date of option exercise.

HOW TO MAKE THE ELECTION

Under U.S. Treasury Regulation 1.83-2(c), the optionee makes an election under IRC Section 83(b) by filing two copies of a written statement with the Internal Revenue Service office with whom he files his individual income tax return (IRS Form 1040). He files the first copy not later than 30 days after the date of option exercise. He files the second copy by attaching it to his income tax return for the taxable year in which the option is exercised.

Under U.S. Treasury Regulation 1.83-2(d), the optionee must also submit a copy of the statement to the corporation *for which he performed services* that led to the granting of the option.

In some cases, the corporation that *grants* the option is different from the corporation that engages the services of the optionee. If so, the optionee must also submit a copy of the statement to the corporation that *granted* the option.

Example: Susan performs services for ABC Corporation, a subsidiary of DEF Corporation. DEF Corporation grants an option to Susan as compensation for services that she provides to ABC Corporation. Susan must submit a copy of the statement to ABC

Corporation (the corporation for which she performed services) *and* to DEF Corporation (the corporation that granted the option).

THE STATEMENT

U.S. Treasury Regulation 1.83-2(e) provides that the statement must be signed by the person making the election and that it state that an election is being made under Internal Revenue Code Section 83(b). The statement must also contain the following information:

- The name, address and taxpayer identification number (social security number) of the taxpayer

- A description of each property with respect to which the election is being made

- The date or dates on which the property is transferred and the taxable year (for example, "calendar year 1999") for which such election is made

- The nature of the restriction or restrictions to which the property is subject

- The fair market value at the time of transfer (determined without regard to any lapse restriction, as defined in Regulation 1.83-3(i)) of each property with respect to which the election is being made

- The amount (if any) paid for such property

- A statement to the effect that copies have been furnished to other persons as provided in Regulation 1.83-2(d)

ELECTION STATEMENT
UNDER INTERNAL REVENUE CODE SECTION 83(b)

Taxpayer name: Lauren Optionee
Address: 111 Apple Court
                               San Rafael, CA. 94903

Taxpayer ID number: 012-34-5678

Description of property: One share of common stock of XYZ Corporation acquired by exercising a nonqualified stock option on December 27, Year 1.

Date of property transfer: December 27, Year 1

Taxable year for which election is being made: Calendar Year 1

Nature of the restriction: As an officer of XYZ Corporation, securities law prohibited me from selling shares of stock during the period December 27, Year 1 through January 15, Year 2.

Fair market value of stock on date of transfer: $100

Amount paid to purchase the stock: $70

I have furnished copies of this statement to persons as required by U.S. Treasury Regulation 1.83-2(d).

_____   _____
Lauren Optionee   Date

3

Incentive Stock Options

This chapter explains the *federal* income tax consequences with respect to transactions that involve incentive stock options. Although *state* income tax law often works in tandem with federal law, often is different from always.

The optionee is *never* taxed on the date that a corporation *grants* him an ISO. He is *never* taxed on the date of ISO *exercise* – for purposes of the regular income tax. He is *always* taxed on the date of option exercise – for purposes of alternative minimum tax (AMT).

In contrast with nonqualified stock options, the optionee is *not* subject to federal income tax *withholding* nor to social security or medicare tax – either on the date of ISO exercise, or on the date that he sells stock previously acquired by ISO exercise.

For regular income tax purposes, the optionee recognizes gain (or loss, in the event that the stock price on the date of sale is less than the option exercise price) on the date that he *sells* the stock. On the date that he sells the stock, he also realizes some sort of income tax consequences for purposes of AMT.

If he sells the stock in the *same* calendar year that he exercises the ISO, the income tax consequences are the same for regular income tax purposes as they are for purposes of alternative minimum tax. If the sale of stock does *not* occur in the calendar year that he exercises the ISO, the amount of income subject to tax in the year of sale for purposes of regular tax is *always* greater than or equal to the amount subject to tax in the year of sale for purposes of AMT.

In order to receive preferential income tax treatment on long-term capital gain from the sale of stock that was previously acquired by exercise of an incentive stock option, the optionee must satisfy two holding periods. The date of disposition must be more than 12 months after the date of ISO exercise, _and_ more than two years after the option's grant date.

Under current tax law, individual taxpayers pay the _greater_ of the regular income tax or tentative AMT. The alternative minimum tax is an important issue for optionees that exercise ISOs but do _not_ sell the stock during the same calendar year.

If the exercise of an ISO _does_ trigger AMT, however, tax law provides an AMT _credit_ against regular tax in years subsequent to the year of ISO exercise – but only to the extent that regular tax exceeds tentative AMT. The AMT credit changes the conventional approach to AMT planning.

IMPORTANT DATES

GRANT DATE

The recipient of an ISO does _not_ recognize taxable income for purposes of either the regular tax or the alternative minimum tax (AMT) on the date that the option is granted.

EXERCISE DATE

The optionee does _not_ recognize taxable income, for purposes of the _regular_ income tax, when he exercises an ISO. For purposes of AMT, however, the excess of the fair market value of the stock acquired by ISO exercise over the exercise price _is_ treated as an item of adjustment and included in the computation of the optionee's alternative minimum taxable income in the year of exercise.

Example: See Table 3.1. On January 10, Year 1, Carol exercises ISOs. The exercise price is $1,000. The fair market value of the stock on the date of exercise is $3,000. Carol does *not* sell the stock in Year 1.

For purposes of AMT, Carol recognizes $2,000 of taxable income in Year 1, the excess of the fair market value of the stock over the exercise price. She does *not* recognize *any* income in Year 1 for purposes of the regular income tax.

Table 3.1

Income Tax Consequences in Year 1
For Purposes of AMT Only

Exercise Date:	January 10, Year 1
Exercise Price:	$1,000
FMV on Exercise Date:	$3,000

Fair market value of stock on exercise date	$3,000
Less: exercise price	1,000
AMT taxable income in Year 1	$2,000
Basis in 100 shares of stock for AMT purposes	$3,000[1]

[1] For AMT purposes, the basis of the stock equals fair market value on date of option exercise ($3,000). For regular tax purposes, the basis equals the exercise price of the option ($1,000).

INCOME TAX WITHHOLDING AND EMPLOYMENT TAXATION

Even though the exercise of an ISO triggers the recognition of taxable income for purposes of AMT, federal income tax withholding is *not* required. Neither is the AMT taxable income subject to social security tax or medicare tax withholding.

DISPOSITION DATE

The *sale* of stock previously acquired by exercise of an ISO is always a taxable event for both the regular income tax and the alternative minimum tax.

The disposition *date* is important because it is used to determine whether the disposition is classified under the Internal Revenue Code as *non-disqualifying* or *disqualifying*. The income tax consequences of this important distinction are discussed later in this chapter.

If the disposition date is more than two years after the option's grant date *and* more than 12 months after the date of option exercise, the disposition is *non*-disqualifying. The disposition is disqualifying if the disposition does *not* satisfy *both* holding period requirements.

INCOME TAX CONSEQUENCES IN TWO DIFFERENT YEARS

If the optionee exercises ISOs and sells the stock in the *same* year, there are federal income tax consequences in that one year only.

If the optionee exercises ISOs in one year but sells the stock in *another*, however, there are income tax consequences in *both* tax years – the calendar year of ISO exercise and the calendar year in which the stock is sold. Not only are there income tax consequences in both tax years, but the tax treatment for AMT purposes and for regular tax purposes is *different* for *both* years.

WHAT *IS*, AND *ISN'T*, A DISPOSITION?

While the *sale* of stock is the most common type of disposition, other transactions involving stock, which was previously acquired by exercise of an ISO, can trigger federal income taxation.

Internal Revenue Code Section 424(c)(1) provides that a disposition includes an *exchange* (with some exceptions), a *gift* or *transfer of legal title*. It also includes the termination of a joint tenancy to the extent that someone other than the optionee acquires ownership of such stock.

The following are *not* dispositions of stock:

- transfer of the stock from a decedent to an estate or a transfer by bequest or inheritance

- certain exchanges (for example, those that involve exchanges of stock and securities in certain types of corporate reorganizations)

- the mere pledge or hypothecation of the stock

- transfer of the stock to a spouse, or to a former spouse if the transfer is incident to the divorce

- registration of the stock in the name of both spouses if the employee lives in a community property state

NON-DISQUALIFYING DISPOSITION

As discussed earlier, in order for the sale of stock previously acquired by ISO exercise to be characterized for income tax purposes as a *non-disqualifying disposition*, the date of disposition must be:

- more than two years after the date of option grant, *and*

- more than 12 months after the date of option exercise

INCOME TAX CONSEQUENCES IN THE YEAR OF SALE

The optionee *never* recognizes *ordinary* income in the year of sale *if* the sale is non-disqualifying. Gain or loss is *always* taxed as *long-term* capital gain or loss. The *amount* of that gain or loss, however, is calculated differently for purposes of the regular tax than for purposes of AMT.

Regular income tax: The optionee recognizes a long-term capital gain or loss in the year of sale. The amount of that gain or loss is equal to the difference between the amount received in the disposition and the exercise price (basis). See Table 3.2.

AMT: The optionee recognizes a long-term capital gain or loss in the year of sale. The amount of that gain or loss is equal to the difference between the amount received in the disposition and the fair market value of the stock (basis) on the date of option exercise. Consequently, the amount of income that the optionee recognizes in the year of sale, for purposes of the regular income tax, is greater than or equal to the amount of income that he recognizes for purposes of AMT. See Table 3.2.

Table 3.2
Long-term Capital Gain or Loss on *Non*-disqualifying Disposition of Stock

Regular Income Tax	Alternative Minimum Tax
Amount received Less: *exercise price*	Amount received Less: *fair market value* on exercise date

---

COMPUTATION OF <u>LONG-TERM</u> CAPITAL GAIN (OR LOSS) IN YEAR OF SALE

Example: Carol exercises ISOs on January 10, Year 1 and pays $1,000 to acquire the stock. On January 11, Year 2, she sells the stock for $3,200. The date of sale is more than two years after the option grant date.

The disposition is *non*-disqualifying because Carol has satisfied both holding period requirements. The date of sale occurs more than 12 months after the date of option exercise *and* more than two years after the date of option grant.

Table 3.3 shows the computation of the $2,200 long-term capital gain in Year 2 for *regular income tax* purposes.

Table 3.4 shows the computation of the $200 long-term capital gain in Year 2 for *alternative minimum tax* purposes.

Notice in Table 3.3 that Carol recognizes a $2,200 long-term capital gain for regular tax purposes. That gain is $2,000 more than

Table 3.3
(see Chart 3.3)

Non-disqualifying Disposition
Income Tax Consequences in Year 2
(for Purposes of *Regular Income Tax*)

Exercise Date:	January 10, Year 1
Sale Date:	January 11, Year 2
Exercise Price:	$1,000
FMV on Exercise Date:	$3,000
Sales Proceeds:	$3,200

Amount received from sale of stock	$3,200
Less: exercise price	1,000
Long-term capital gain in Year 2	$2,200

Table 3.4
(see Chart 3.4)

Non-disqualifying Disposition
Income Tax Consequences in Year 2
(for Purposes of *Alternative Minimum Tax*)

Exercise Date:	January 10, Year 1
Sale Date:	January 11, Year 2
Exercise Price:	$1,000
FMV on Exercise Date:	$3,000
Sales Proceeds:	$3,200

Amount received from sale of stock	$3,200
Less: FMV of stock on date of exercise	3,000
Long-term capital gain in Year 2	$ 200

Chart 3.3
(see Table 3.3)

Income Tax Consequences in Year 2
(for Purposes of Regular Income Tax)

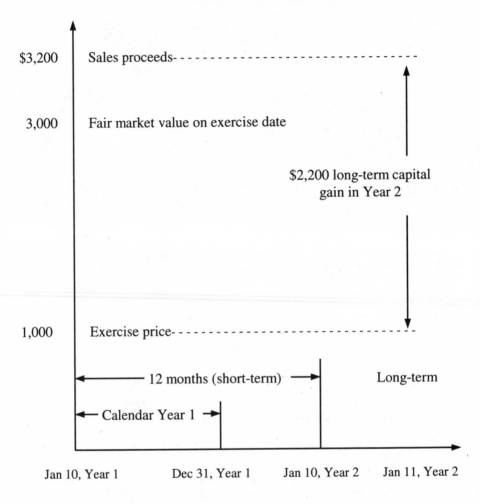

Chart 3.4
(see Table 3.4)

Income Tax Consequences in Year 2
(for Purposes of Alternative Minimum Tax)

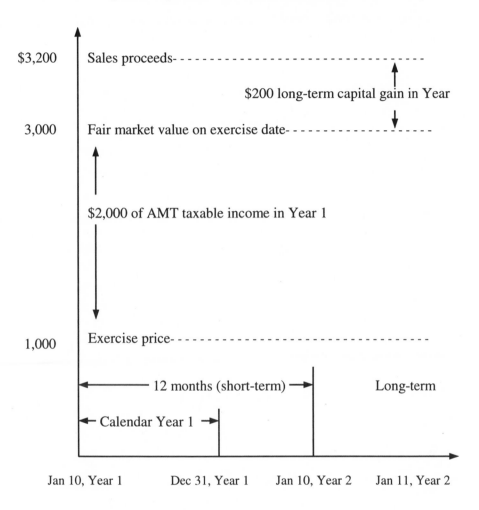

$3,200   Sales proceeds- -

$200 long-term capital gain in Year

3,000   Fair market value on exercise date- -

$2,000 of AMT taxable income in Year 1

1,000   Exercise price- -

  12 months (short-term) →   Long-term

← Calendar Year 1 →

Jan 10, Year 1   Dec 31, Year 1   Jan 10, Year 2   Jan 11, Year 2 the $200 long-term capital gain (Table 3.4) that she recognizes for AMT.

Carol's long-term capital gain is $2,000 *less* for AMT purposes than it is for regular tax purposes because she had previously recognized $2,000 of taxable income for purposes of AMT in the year that she exercised the ISOs (see Table 3.1). The recognition of that income increased her basis in the stock by $2,000 for purposes of AMT.

The *total* amount of income recognized by Carol is the *same* for regular tax purposes as it is for AMT. The *timing* of income recognition is different, however.

For AMT purposes, the optionee recognizes *more* income in the year of exercise and *less* in the year of sale. For regular tax purposes, he recognizes *less* (none) income in the year of exercise and *more* in the year of sale.

> **Unless otherwise stated, all references to exercising ISOs and holding the stock for more than 12 months assume that the optionee also holds the stock for more than two years after option grant date. Therefore, the eventual sale of such stock is characterized for income tax purposes as a non-disqualifying disposition.**

DISQUALIFYING DISPOSITION

If the disposition of stock is *not* a *non*-disqualifying disposition, it is a disqualifying disposition.

When a disposition is disqualifying, the optionee recognizes *ordinary compensation income,* on the date of disposition, to the extent of the *lesser* of:

(a) the difference between the fair market value of such shares on the date of exercise and the exercise price, and

(b) the difference between the amount received in the disposition and the exercise price.

EXERCISE ISO AND SELL STOCK IN SAME CALENDAR YEAR - COMPUTATION OF TAXABLE GAIN IN YEAR OF SALE

When the optionee exercises an ISO and sells the stock in the same calendar year:

- the disposition is always disqualifying, *and*

- the income tax consequences for purposes of the regular tax and alternative minimum tax are the *same*.

This section presents two examples. In the first (Table 3.5), the optionee's gain on the sale of stock consists entirely of *ordinary compensation income* because the fair market value of the stock on the date of sale is *less* than it was on the date of exercise (but the fair market value exceeds the exercise price).

In the second example (Table 3.6), a portion of the optionee's gain is taxed as ordinary compensation income and a portion is taxed as *short-term capital gain* because the fair market value of the stock on the date of sale is *more* than it was on the date of exercise.

Stock Price is Lower on Sale Date than it was on Exercise Date (But the Stock Price is Higher than the Exercise Price)

Example: See Table 3.5. On January 10, Year 1, Carol exercises ISOs to buy 100 shares of stock. The option exercise price is $1,000 ($10 per share) and the fair market value of the stock on the date of exercise is $3,000 ($30 per share). Carol sells the stock for $2,800 on March 5, Year 1.

Disqualifying or non-disqualifying disposition?: The sale of stock is a *disqualifying* disposition because Carol does *not* hold the stock for more than 12 months after the date of option exercise.

Amount of ordinary compensation income: Carol recognizes ordinary compensation income in the amount of the *lesser* of (a) the $2,000 excess of the fair market value ($3,000) of the stock on the date of exercise and the exercise price ($1,000), *and* (b) the $1,800 excess of the amount received in the disposition ($2,800) and the exercise price ($1,000). Consequently, Carol recognizes $1,800 of ordinary compensation income in Year 1.

Amount of capital gain: If the optionee's proceeds from the sale are *more* than what the fair market value of the stock was on the date of ISO exercise, such excess is taxed as capital gain. The gain is taxed as short-term capital gain if the optionee does *not* hold the stock for more than 12 months after the date of option exercise.

In this example, the $2,800 proceeds from the sale are *not* more than the $3,000 fair market value of the stock on the date of exercise. Therefore, Carol does *not* recognize *any* short-term capital gain on the date of sale.

Withholding: Under IRS Notice 87-49, gain from the sale of stock acquired by ISO exercise is *not* subject to income tax withholding, and *not* subject to social security or medicare tax.

Stock Price is <u>Higher</u> on Sale Date than it was on Exercise Date

Example: See Table 3.6. Instead of selling the stock for $2,800 (as shown in Table 3.5), Carol sells the stock for $3,200. Her total gain is $2,200, the excess of the $3,200 received from the sale of stock over the $1,000 exercise price.

Notice in Table 3.6 that Carol recognizes *both* ordinary compensation income *and* capital gain in the year of sale. This occurs because the stock price on the date of sale is *higher* than it was on the date of exercise.

Amount of ordinary compensation income: Carol recognizes $2,000 of ordinary compensation income, the *lesser* of **A** ($2,000) or **B** ($2,200).

Amount of capital gain: Carol also recognizes short-term capital gain in the amount of $200, the excess of his $2,200 total gain over the $2,000 that he recognizes as ordinary compensation income. The gain is short-term because the March 5, Year 1 date of sale is not more than 12 months after the January 10, Year 1 date of ISO exercise.

Table 3.5
(see Chart 3.5)

Disqualifying Disposition
Income Tax Consequences in Year 1

Exercise Date:	January 10, Year 1
Sale Date:	March 5, Year 1
Exercise Price:	$1,000
FMV on Exercise Date:	$3,000
Sales Proceeds:	$2,800

Fair market value of stock on exercise date	$3,000	
Less: exercise price	1,000	
Excess of fair market value over option price	$2,000	A
Amount received from sale of stock	$2,800	
Less: exercise price	1,000	
Excess of amount received over exercise price	$1,800	B
Ordinary compensation income (lesser of A and B)	$1,800	

Stock Price is _Lower_ than the Exercise Price

In the unfortunate circumstance where the stock is sold at a price that is *less* than the exercise price, IRC Section 422(c)(2) provides that the optionee does *not* recognize *any* ordinary income on the disposition.

The optionee realizes a capital *loss*. The loss is taxed as a short-term capital loss because the date of sale is *not* more than 12 months after the date of ISO exercise. The amount of the loss is equal to the difference between the proceeds from the sale and the exercise price (his basis in the stock).

Chart 3.5
(see Table 3.5)

Income Tax Consequences in Year 1
(for Purposes of Regular Income Tax and AMT)

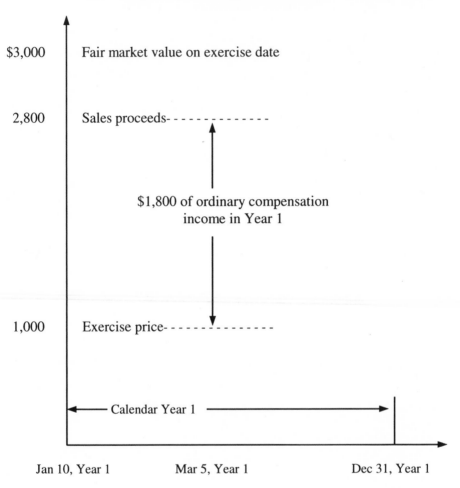

$3,000   Fair market value on exercise date

2,800   Sales proceeds- - - - - - - - - - - - - -

$1,800 of ordinary compensation
income in Year 1

1,000   Exercise price- - - - - - - - - - - - - -

Calendar Year 1

Jan 10, Year 1   Mar 5, Year 1   Dec 31, Year 1

Example: Carol exercises ISOs on January 10, Year 1. The exercise price is $1,000. She sells the stock on December 10, Year 1 for $900.

Carol does not recognize any ordinary compensation income. She realizes a short-term capital loss in the amount of $100, the difference between the $900 proceeds and the $1,000 exercise price.

Regular income tax and AMT: The income tax consequences are the *same* for both regular income tax purposes and for AMT because the ISO exercise and the sale of stock occur during the same calendar year.

Table 3.6

Disqualifying Disposition
Income Tax Consequences in Year 1

Exercise Date:	January 10, Year 1
Sale Date:	March 5, Year 1
Exercise Price:	$1,000
FMV on Exercise Date:	$3,000
Sales Proceeds:	$3,200

Fair market value of stock on exercise date	$3,000	
Less: exercise price	1,000	
Excess of fair market value over exercise price	$2,000	A
Amount received from sale of stock	$3,200	
Less: exercise price	1,000	
Excess of amount received over exercise price	$2,200	B
Ordinary compensation income (lesser of A and B)	$2,000	
Short-term capital gain	200	
Total gain recognized in Year 1	$2,200	

EXERCISE ISO IN ONE CALENDAR YEAR AND SELL STOCK IN A DIFFERENT CALENDAR YEAR - COMPUTATION OF TAXABLE GAIN IN YEAR OF SALE

When the optionee exercises an ISO in one calendar year but sells the stock in *another* calendar year:

- the sale of stock may or may not be a disqualifying disposition

- the tax consequences for purposes of the regular income tax and AMT are different

- the total amount of income recognized in the year of sale for purposes of the regular income tax is always greater than or equal to the amount recognized for AMT

- one hundred percent of any gain or loss in the year of sale, for purposes of AMT, is taxed as *capital* gain or loss – short or long-term depending upon whether or not the optionee holds the stock more than 12 months after the ISO exercise date

As discussed earlier, the sale of stock is a disqualifying disposition if *either* of two holding period requirements is not satisfied. Either the optionee does not hold the stock for more than 12 months after the date of ISO exercise *or* the sale date is not more than two years after the option's grant date.

This section describes the federal income tax consequences that result from a disqualifying disposition of stock that occurs in a year *subsequent* to the calendar year of ISO exercise.

The *total* amount of income that the optionee recognizes in the year of sale, for regular income tax purposes, is always greater than or equal to the total amount of income that he recognizes for AMT. This occurs because the optionee previously recognized income in the year of ISO exercise, for AMT purposes, in the amount of the excess of the fair market value of the stock on the date of exercise over the exercise price.

Example: Carol exercises ISOs on January 10, Year 1 and pays $1,000 to acquire the stock. The fair market value of the stock on the date of exercise is $3,000. On January 5, Year 2, she sells the stock for $3,200. See Tables 3.7 and 3.8.

The disposition is disqualifying because the January 5, Year 2 date of sale is not more than 12 months after the January 10, Year 1 date of option exercise.

In a disqualifying disposition that occurs *subsequent* to the calendar year of exercise, the amount of income that is subject to tax is *different* for regular tax purposes than for AMT purposes.

Table 3.7 shows the computation of ordinary compensation income, and short-term capital gain, in Year 2 (the year of sale) for *regular income tax* purposes. The total amount of income subject to regular tax is $2,200, some of which is taxed as ordinary income ($2,000) and some as short-term capital gain ($200).

Table 3.8 shows the computation of short-term capital gain in Year 2 for *alternative minimum tax* purposes. Notice that the *total* amount of income subject to AMT in the year of *sale* is only $200 (versus $2,200 for regular tax) because Carol had already recognized $2,000 of taxable income in the year of *exercise,* for purposes of AMT.

SALES PRICE IS LOWER THAN THE EXERCISE PRICE

In the unfortunate circumstance where the stock price declines after the date of ISO exercise and the amount received in the disposition is *less* than the exercise price, IRC Section 422(c)(2) provides that the optionee does *not* recognize *any* ordinary income on the disposition. He realizes a *capital loss* in the year of sale.

Example: Carol exercises ISOs on January 10, Year 1. The exercise price is $1,000 and the fair market value of the stock on the date of exercise is $3,000. She sells the stock on January 5, Year 2 for $900.

Regular income tax: Carol does *not* recognize *any* ordinary compensation income. She realizes a capital *loss* in the year of sale in the amount of $100, the difference between the $900 proceeds from the sale and the $1,000 exercise price (her basis for regular income tax purposes).

The loss is taxed as a *short-term* capital loss because the January 5, Year 2 date of sale is *not* more than 12 months after the January 10, Year 1 date of exercise.

Table 3.7
(see Chart 3.7)

<u>Disqualifying Disposition</u>
Income Tax Consequences in Year 2
(for Purposes of the *Regular Income Tax*)

Exercise Date:	**January 10, Year 1**
Sale Date:	**January 5, Year 2**
Exercise Price:	**$1,000**
FMV on Exercise Date:	**$3,000**
Sales Proceeds:	**$3,200**

Fair market value of stock on exercise date	$3,000	
Less: exercise price	<u>1,000</u>	
Excess of fair market value over exercise price	<u>$2,000</u>	**A**
Amount received from sale of stock	$3,200	
Less: exercise price	<u>1,000</u>	
Excess of amount received over exercise price	<u>$2,200</u>	**B**
Ordinary compensation income (lesser of **A** and **B**)	<u>$2,000</u>	
Short-term capital gain	<u>200</u>	
Total gain recognized in Year 2	<u>$2,200</u>	

AMT: For purposes of the alternative minimum tax, Carol does not recognize any ordinary compensation income.

She realizes a short-term capital loss in the year of sale in the amount of $2,100, the difference between the $900 proceeds from the sale and the $3,000 fair market value of the stock on the date of ISO exercise (her basis for AMT purposes).

Chart 3.7
(see Table 3.7)

Income Tax Consequences in Year 2
(for Purposes of Regular Income Tax)

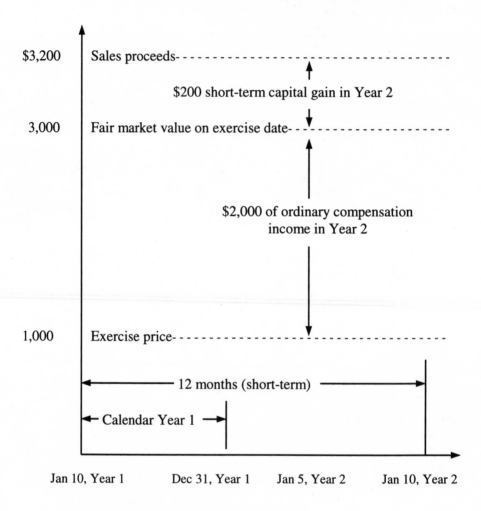

Chart 3.8
(see Table 3.8)

Income Tax Consequences in Year 2
(for Purposes of Alternative Minimum Tax)

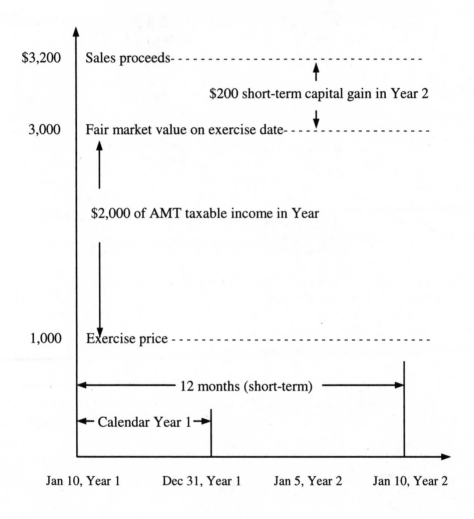

Table 3.8
(see Chart 3.8)

Disqualifying Disposition
Income Tax Consequences in Year 2
(for Purposes of *Alternative Minimum Tax*)

Exercise Date:	January 10, Year 1
Sale Date:	January 5, Year 2
Exercise Price:	$1,000
FMV on Exercise Date:	$3,000
Sales Proceeds:	$3,200

Amount received from sale of stock	$3,200
Less: basis of stock sold	3,000[1]
Short-term capital gain in Year 2	$ 200

[1] basis for purposes of AMT equals the fair market value of the stock on the date of ISO exercise

---

INCOME TAX WITHHOLDING AND EMPLOYMENT TAXATION

Gain on a disqualifying disposition is *not* subject to federal income tax *withholding* - and *not* subject to social security or medicare tax.

ALTERNATIVE MINIMUM TAX

In the 1970s, Congress passed legislation that established a minimum tax. Under current law, the U.S. Internal Revenue Code provides that the individual taxpayer pays the *greater* of the tentative alternative minimum tax or the regular income tax.

THE ISO ADJUSTMENT AND THE AMT CREDIT

The alternative minimum tax *credit* helps to ensure (but does not *guarantee*) that optionees do not pay *both* regular tax *and* AMT on gain that results from an ISO exercise and sale of stock.

AMT becomes an issue when the optionee exercises an ISO but does not sell the stock in the same calendar year. If the optionee exercises ISOs and does *not* sell the stock in the same calendar year, the ISO exercise results in an AMT adjustment that the optionee reports on IRS Form 6251 - for the tax year in which the ISO is exercised.

That ISO adjustment is included in the computation of alternative minimum taxable income. It may, or may not, trigger AMT.

Example: Optionees A, B and C file *joint* income tax returns with their spouses. All three optionees exercise ISOs when the fair market value of the stock on the date of exercise exceeds the option exercise price by $20,000. None of the three sells the stock during the calendar year of exercise.

Since they don't sell the stock during the year of exercise, they each generate a $20,000 AMT adjustment that is reported as taxable income, for AMT purposes, on IRS Form 6251. The $20,000 adjustment affects each taxpayer *differently*. See Table 3.9.

OPTIONEE A

See Table 3.9. The $97,860 of tentative AMT does *not* exceed the $100,284 of regular tax. Since tentative AMT is *not* greater than regular tax, AMT equals zero. Consequently, the ISO adjustment triggers $0 of AMT for Optionee A and her spouse.

OPTIONEE B

See Table 3.9. Since the $97,860 of tentative AMT exceeds the regular tax by $744, AMT equals $744. In other words, AMT is simply the excess of tentative AMT over the regular income tax.

If Optionee B did *not* have the $20,000 adjustment, she and her spouse would pay $0 of AMT (see "AMT without ISO adjustment" in Table 3.9). Because of the $20,000 ISO adjustment, however, they incur $744 of AMT. In effect, then, the $20,000 adjustment triggers $744 of AMT.

Optionee B and her spouse receive a $744 AMT credit. They may use it to reduce regular tax in *subsequent* years, but only to the extent that their regular tax liability in those years exceeds tentative AMT. They claim the credit on next year's IRS Form 8801. If they can't utilize the entire credit next year, they apply the unused amount to the following year. This process of carrying the credit forward continues indefinitely until the AMT credit is fully utilized.

OPTIONEE C

See Table 3.9. Since the $97,860 of tentative AMT exceeds the regular tax by $7,476, AMT equals $7,476. In other words, AMT is simply the excess of tentative AMT over the regular income tax.

If C did *not* have the adjustment, she and her spouse would pay $1,876 of AMT (see "AMT without ISO adjustment" in Table 3.9). In effect, then, the $20,000 adjustment triggers $5,600 ($7,476 minus $1,876) of AMT. Optionee C and her spouse pay AMT tax at the rate of 28 percent (28% x $20,000 equals $5,600) on the ISO adjustment.

Optionee C and her spouse receive a $5,600 AMT credit.

DEFERRAL VERSUS EXCLUSION ITEMS

The ISO adjustment is termed a *deferral* item, as opposed to an *exclusion* item. Exclusion items include state income taxes, real estate and personal property taxes, tax consulting and preparation fees, and other miscellaneous itemized deductions that taxpayers report on IRS Form 1040, Schedule A *"Itemized Deductions"*.

While an exclusion item results in a *permanent* difference in taxable income over time, a deferral item does *not* result in a permanent difference in taxable income over time. A deferral item results in a *timing* difference which can cause the taxpayer to pay more income tax now, and less later - by operation of the AMT.

The *disadvantage* of paying more tax now, and less later, is that money has a time value. One dollar of income tax paid now is more costly than one dollar paid later.

Table 3.9			
The $20,000 ISO Adjustment Affects Optionees A, B & C Differently			
	A	**B**	**C**
Total income	$375,000	$375,000	$375,000
Less:state taxes	31,500	39,500	56,500
Less:other deductions	25,386	25,386	25,386
Less:exemptions	0	0	0
Regular taxable income	318,114	310,114	293,114
Regular tax	100,284	97,116	90,384
Tentative AMT	97, 860	97,860	97,860
AMT⇒	0	744	7,476
AMT w/o ISO adjustment⇒	0	0	1,876
AMT credit carryforward⇒	0	744	5,600
Note: tax computations are based upon 1997 income tax rates			

With respect to the previous example, Optionee B and her spouse, in effect, make a $744 *interest-free loan* to the U.S. Treasury. That "loan" will be repaid (via the AMT credit) when, or *if*, and to the extent that their regular income tax liability in tax years subsequent to the year of ISO exercise exceeds their tentative AMT. Optionee C and her spouse make a $5,600 loan to the U.S. Treasury under the same unfavorable terms.

AMT Planning is Different

Corporate executives engage the services of tax professionals and pay them substantial fees to design strategies that minimize or eliminate AMT.

Objective: Equalize Tentative AMT and Regular Tax

Generally, when *exclusion* items trigger AMT, the tax planning strategy is to accelerate ordinary income into the current tax year. For example, a sole proprietor who reports taxable income on the cash method of accounting tries to accelerate income by invoicing customers on December 1 (because he wants to be paid *on or before* December 31) rather than waiting until December 15.

The taxpayer tries to accelerate just enough ordinary income so that tentative AMT equals regular tax. Since AMT is equal to the *excess* of tentative AMT over regular tax, AMT equals *zero* when tentative AMT equals regular tax. That's the objective of AMT planning - *when exclusion items trigger AMT.*

By accelerating ordinary income into a year when the taxpayer is otherwise subject to AMT, the income that is accelerated is effectively taxed at the lower AMT rate of either 26 or 28 percent (although the effective rate is higher than 26 or 28 percent if the additional income causes a reduction in the exemption amount).

This strategy can be particularly attractive when the taxpayer's marginal federal rate for regular tax purposes is substantially higher than the marginal tax rate on alternative minimum taxable income.

Tax Planning Differs when an ISO Exercise Triggers AMT

The AMT credit that arises when an ISO adjustment triggers AMT *changes* the approach to conventional AMT planning.

In the example that follows, Optionee B does *not* use the conventional strategy of AMT planning. Optionee B does *not* accelerate income into Year 1 in order to avoid AMT in Year 1.

Instead, she wisely chooses to pay AMT in Year 1. The $744 of AMT that she and her spouse incur, results in a $744 AMT tax *credit.* They utilize that $744 AMT credit in Year 2 to reduce their *regular* income tax liability.

Example: Recall from Table 3.9 that Optionee B exercises ISOs in Year 1. The exercise results in $744 of AMT in Year 1 and a $744 AMT credit carryforward to Year 2.

Table 3.10 shows the federal income tax consequences in Years 1 and 2 if Optionee B *accelerates* $6,258 of income from her sole proprietorship into Year 1 in order to avoid AMT in Year 1.

Table 3.11 shows the federal income tax consequences in Years 1 and 2 if Optionee B does *not* accelerate income into Year 1. Instead, she receives the income that she *could* have received in Year 1, if she had sent invoices to clients early in December, in Year 2.

Table 3.12 compares the cash flows that result from each of the two alternatives.

Whichever strategy she chooses, Optionee B and her spouse pay $197,488 in *total* federal tax over the two-year period. If she accelerates income, they pay *more* tax in Year 1 ($100,372) and *less* in Year 2 ($97,116). If she does *not* accelerate income, they pay *less* tax in Year 1 ($97,860) and *more* in Year 2 ($99,628).

An analysis of the differential cash flows (column 3 of Table 3.12) reveals that *not* accelerating income is the wiser strategy. In fact, it would be difficult to find many rational, informed investors that *would* choose to receive the cash flows associated with Table 3.12 column A over those in column B. The higher the rates of return on alternative investment opportunities, the less attractive it is for Optionee B to accelerate income into Year 1.

Table 3.10

Optionee B Accelerates $6,258 of Schedule C Income into Year 1 to Avoid AMT in Year 1

	Year 1	Year 2
Total income	$381,258	375,000
Less: 1/2 of self-employment tax	442	0
Adjusted gross income	$380,816	375,000
Less:itemized deductions	64,712	64,886
Regular taxable income	$316,104	310,114
Regular income tax	99,488[1]	97,116[2]
Self-employment tax	884	0
Alternative minimum tax	0[1]	0[2]
Total federal tax	$100,372	97,116
Less: federal withholding	100,000	100,000
Refund (balance due) per Form 1040	(372)	2,884

[1] tentative AMT equals $99,488; regular income tax equals $99,488; Optionee pays the *greater* of tentative AMT or regular income tax. Therefore, AMT equals $0, the excess of tentative AMT over regular income tax

[2] tentative AMT equals $92,260; regular income tax equals $97,116; Therefore, AMT equals $0, the excess of tentative AMT over regular income tax

Assumptions:

a) 1997 income tax rates
b) income tax rates in Years 1 and 2 are the same
c) $6,258 of Schedule C income is received on December 15, Year 1 and no Schedule C income is received during Year 2

Table 3.11

Optionee B Does Not Accelerate Any Schedule C Income into Year 1. She Pays AMT in Year 1 and Receives an AMT Credit That Reduces Regular Tax in Year 2

	Year 1	Year 2
Total income	$375,000	381,258
Less: 1/2 of self-employment tax	0	442
Adjusted gross income	$375,000	380,816
Less:itemized deductions	64,886	64,712
Regular taxable income	$310,114	316,104
Regular income tax	97,116[1]	99,488[2]
Less: AMT credit against regular tax	0	744
Regular income tax after credits	97,116	98,744
Plus: self-employment tax	0	884
Plus: alternative minimum tax	744[1]	0[2]
Total federal tax	$ 97,860	99,628
Less: federal withholding	100,000	100,000
Refund (balance due) per Form 1040	2,140	372

[1] tentative AMT equals $97,860; regular income tax equals $97,116; Optionee pays the *greater* of tentative AMT or regular income tax. Therefore, AMT equals $744, the excess of tentative AMT over regular income tax

[2] tentative AMT equals $93,888; regular income tax equals $99,488; Therefore, AMT equals $0, the excess of tentative AMT over regular income tax

Assumptions:

a) 1997 income tax rates
b) income tax rates in Years 1 and 2 are the same
c) Optionee B does not receive any Schedule C income during Year 1. He receives $6,258 of Schedule C income on January 15, Year 2.

Table 3.12

Comparison of Cash Flows (See Tables 3.10 and 3.11) Accelerate versus Not Accelerate Income into Year 1

Date	(A) Accelerate	(B) Not Accelerate	(A) - (B) Difference
Dec 15, Year 1	$6,258[1]	0	$6,258
Jan 15, Year 2	0	6,258[1]	(6,258)
Apr 15, Year 2	(372)[2]	2,140[3]	(2,512)
Apr 15, Year 3	2,884[4]	372[4]	2,512
	$8,770	8,770	0

[1] Optionee B's sole proprietorship receives $6,258 for services provided
[2] Payable to Internal Revenue Service per IRS Form 1040 for the year ended December 31, Year 1
[3] Refund from the Internal Revenue Service per IRS Form 1040 for the year ended December 31, Year 1
[4] Refund from the Internal Revenue Service per IRS Form 1040 for the year ended December 31, Year 2

4

Tax-deferred Exchanges

At the time of ISO exercise, the optionee may pay for shares in cash or with a promissory note. Tax law also permits a cashless exercise (followed by a same-day sale of stock) and a tax-deferred exchange under Internal Revenue Code Section 1036.

The general rule under IRC Section 1036 is that "No gain or loss shall be recognized if common stock in a corporation is exchanged solely for common stock in the same corporation...". IRC Section 422(c)(4)(A) provides that "the employee may pay for the stock with stock of the corporation granting the option".

If the employer's plan permits, optionees who already own shares may exchange them for shares of the same corporation without triggering a capital gains tax on unrealized capital gain that exists in the shares already owned. In effect, optionees use "old" shares (instead of cash) to pay for "new" shares to be acquired by exercising options - in a *tax-deferred exchange*.

EXERCISING <u>NQSO</u>s AND PAYING WITH STOCK THAT HAD BEEN ACQUIRED BY EXERCISE OF A NONQUALIFIED STOCK OPTION

The following example shows how an optionee exercises nonqualified stock options (NQSOs) and uses shares of stock that he already owns as payment of the exercise price – *without* triggering an income tax liability on any of the appreciation in the shares that he already owns.

Example: The current price of ABC stock is $5 per share. On December 10, Year 1, Patricia wants to exercise *NQSOs* that give her the right to purchase 100 shares of her employer's stock (ABC Corporation) at an exercise price of $1 per share. She prefers to effect the exercise without using cash.

She already owns shares: Pat owns 20 shares of ABC stock that have a current fair market value of $100. She acquired the shares on January 2, Year 1 by exercising *NQSOs*. Her exercise price was $1 per share ($20). The fair market value of ABC stock on the date of exercise was $3 per share ($60).

Basis of 20 "old" shares: The basis of the 20 shares is $60, their fair market value on the date she exercised the NQSOs.

If she sells 20 "old" shares to raise cash: If she sells the 20 old shares at $5 per share, her gross proceeds are $100. Her basis is $60. She pays income tax on a $40 short-term capital gain. The gain would be short-term because the December 10, Year 1 date of sale is not more than 12 months after the January 2, Year 1 date of acquisition. She doesn't like this alternative because the sale of stock triggers an income tax liability. Instead, she makes a tax-deferred exchange of 20 "old" shares for 100 "new" shares.

Tax-deferred exchange: On December 10, Year 1, Patricia exercises NQSOs on 100 shares of stock (at an exercise price of $1 per share). She pays the $100 exercise price by surrendering 20 "old" shares, which have a fair market value of $100, to ABC Corporation. In exchange for the 20 "old" shares, she receives 100 "new" shares from ABC Corporation. No cash is required.

Taxable gain: Patricia recognizes $400 of ordinary compensation income on December 10, Year 1, the date of NQSO exercise. That taxable gain is equal to the excess of the $500 ($5 per share) fair market value of the shares on the date of exercise over the $100 ($1 per share) exercise price.

Basis of 100 "new" shares: She now holds 100 "new" shares. IRC Section 1031(d) provides that if property is acquired in an exchange described in IRC Section 1036(a), the basis of that property shall be the same as that of the property exchanged. Therefore, as discussed in IRS Private Letter Ruling 9629028, Patricia's basis in 20 of the "new" shares is $60 (the same as her basis in the 20 "old" shares that she surrenders). Patricia's basis in 80 of the "new" shares is $400, the amount of taxable compensation income she recognizes on the exercise of the nonqualified stock options. Her total basis in the 100 shares is $460.

Acquisition date for computing holding period: Under IRC Section 1223, the date of acquisition on 20 of the "new" shares, for purposes of computing her holding period, is January 2, Year 1, the date she originally acquired the 20 "old" shares. The date of acquisition on 80 of the "new" shares begins on December 10, Year 1, the date she exercises the NQSOs on 100 shares of stock.

Summary: The stock-for-stock exchange under Internal Revenue Code Section 1036 allows Patricia to use the $100 fair market value of stock she currently owns to pay the $100 exercise price to acquire the 100 new shares - without paying income tax on the $40 of unrealized appreciation in the "old" shares.

SURRENDERING SHARES PREVIOUSLY ACQUIRED THROUGH THE EXERCISE OF AN ISO OR THROUGH PARTICIPATION IN A QUALIFIED STOCK PURCHASE PLAN

In the above stock-for-stock example, Patricia exchanges 20 "old" shares of stock which she previously acquired by exercising a *nonqualified* stock option.

The federal income tax consequences are different if the 20 "old" shares had been acquired (1) by exercising an incentive stock option *or* (2) via participation in a qualified stock purchase plan, <u>and</u> (3) applicable holding period requirements are *not* met *before* surrendering the "old" shares. In this situation, the surrender of the "old" shares is treated as a disqualifying disposition.

If the applicable holding periods for stock acquired by ISO exercise (more than 12 months after exercise date *and* more than two years after grant date) on the 20 shares *have* been satisfied, however, the stock-for-stock exchange defers the recognition of the $40 of appreciation in the 20 shares which are surrendered.

EXERCISING ISOS AND PAYING WITH MATURE ISO STOCK

Mature ISO stock is stock that was previously acquired through the exercise of an incentive stock option and that has satisfied the holding period requirements of IRC Section 422(a). In other words, the optionee has held the stock for more than 12 months, and more than two years have passed since the option's grant date.

The following example shows how an optionee exercises incentive stock options (ISOs) and uses mature ISO stock as payment of the exercise price – without triggering an income tax liability on any of the appreciation in the mature ISO stock.

Example: The current price of ABC stock is $5 per share. On December 10, Year 3, Patricia wants to exercise *ISOs* that give her the right to purchase 100 shares of her employer's stock (ABC Corporation) at an exercise price of $1 per share. She prefers to pay the exercise price without using cash.

She already owns shares: Pat owns 20 shares of ABC stock that she acquired on January 2, Year 1 by exercising *ISOs*. Her exercise price was $1 per share ($20). The fair market value on the date of exercise was $3 per share ($60).

Basis of 20 "old" shares: Patricia's basis for regular tax purposes is $20, the exercise price. Her basis for AMT purposes is $60, the fair market value of the stock on the date of ISO exercise.

If she sells 20 "old" shares: If she sells the 20 shares on December 10, Year 3, she makes a non-disqualifying disposition because she holds the stock for more than 12 months after the January 2, Year 1 exercise date *and* more than two years after the option grant date.

If she sells the 20 shares at $5 per share, her gross proceeds are $100. Her long-term capital gain for regular tax purposes is $80 ($100 FMV - $20 basis). Her long-term capital gain for AMT purposes is $40 ($100 FMV - $60 basis). The gain is long-term because the December 10, Year 3 date of sale is more than 12 months after the January 2, Year 1 date of ISO exercise. She doesn't like this alternative because the sale of stock triggers an income tax liability. Instead, she makes a tax-deferred exchange of 20 "old" shares for 100 "new" shares.

Tax-deferred exchange: On December 10, Year 3, Patricia exercises ISOs on 100 shares of stock (at an exercise price of $1 per share). She pays the $100 exercise price by surrendering 20 old shares, which have a fair market value of $100, to ABC Corporation. The surrender of the 20 shares (which had previously been acquired by exercising ISOs) is *not* a disqualifying disposition because *prior* to the date of surrender she had already satisfied holding period requirements. In exchange for the 20 old shares, she receives 100 new shares from ABC Corporation. No cash is required.

Taxable gain for regular tax purposes: Patricia does not recognize any taxable income for regular tax purposes as a result of the December 10, Year 3 ISO exercise.

Taxable gain for AMT purposes: Patricia recognizes $400 of income in Year 3 for purposes of AMT. That $400 is equal to the excess of the $500 ($5 per share) fair market value of the shares on the date of exercise over the $100 ($1 per share) exercise price.

Basis of 100 "new" shares for regular tax purposes: She now holds 100 "new" shares. IRC Section 1031(d) provides that if property is acquired in an exchange described in IRC Section 1036(a), the basis of that property shall be the same as that of the property exchanged. In accordance with IRS Private Letter Ruling 9629028, Patricia's basis in 20 of the "new" shares is $20 (the same as her basis in the 20 "old" shares that she surrenders). Patricia's basis in 80 of the "new" shares is $0. Her total basis in the 100 shares is $20.

Basis of 100 "new" shares for AMT purposes: She now holds 100 "new" shares. In accordance with IRC Section 1031(d) which provides that the property received shall have the same basis as the property exchanged, and IRS Private Letter Ruling 9629028, Patricia's basis in 20 of the "new" shares is $60 (the same as her basis in the 20 "old" shares that she surrenders). Patricia's basis in 80 of the "new" shares is $400, the amount of taxable compensation income she recognizes on the date that she exercises the ISOs. Her total basis in the 100 shares is $460.

Acquisition date for computing holding period: Under IRC Section 1223, the date of acquisition on 20 of the "new" shares, for purposes of computing her holding period, is January 2, Year 1, the date she originally acquired the 20 "old" shares. The date of acquisition on 80 of the "new" shares begins on December 10, Year 3, the date she exercises the ISOs on 100 shares of stock.

Acquisition date for determining non-disqualifying versus disqualifying disposition: As discussed in Private Letter Ruling 9629028, the holding period for purposes of determining whether the eventual disposition of the 100 shares of "new" stock acquired by ISO exercise is a disqualifying or non-disqualifying disposition begins on December 10, Year 3, the date of ISO exercise. That date applies to *all* 100 shares, not just the 80 additional shares acquired on December 10, Year 3. Consequently, if Pat disposes of shares before December 11, Year 4 the disposition will be treated as disqualifying.

5

Two Tax-saving Strategies (but are they right for you?)

Two of the more common tax-saving strategies that involve compensatory stock options are examined in this chapter. One is the exercise of ISOs and sale of stock 12 months and one day later, the objective of which is to convert ordinary income into long-term capital gain. The other is the early exercise of NQSOs, the objective of which is to convert anticipated appreciation in the stock price after the date of exercise into long-term capital gain.

I. EXERCISE ISOs AND HOLD THE STOCK

In most cases, the relevant question for the ISO holder is: Which projected series of cash flows is likely to offer more value, those that result from:

- Exercising ISOs and selling the stock on the same day, *or*

- Exercising ISOs and selling the stock 12 months and one day after exercise?

TWO CRITICAL CONDITIONS

As a *general rule*, exercising ISOs and selling the stock 12 months and one day after exercise is most appropriate where two conditions are present:

- the optionee is subject to a marginal income tax rate on ordinary income that is *substantially* in *excess* of the tax rate on long-term capital gains, *and*

- the option exercise price is relatively *low* in relation to the fair market value of the stock on the date of exercise.

One should observe that the optionee who is subject to higher marginal income tax rates on ordinary income reaps more of an income tax savings when he converts ordinary income into long-term capital gain than the optionee who is subject to a lower marginal income tax rate on ordinary income.

One should also observe that if the exercise price is relatively low in relation to the fair market value of the stock on the date of exercise it means that the gain is larger. Naturally, the larger the gain, the more the income tax savings on the conversion of that gain from ordinary income into long-term capital gain.

As the excess of the marginal rate on ordinary income over the rate of tax on long-term capital gain *declines*, <u>or</u> as the exercise price as a percentage of the fair market value of the stock *increases*, exercising ISOs and holding the stock for 12 months and one day becomes a less attractive alternative.

In fact, exercising ISOs and holding the stock for 12 months and one day is not a wealth-maximizing strategy for many optionees because the internal rate of return that results from this strategy is sometimes less – and often substantially less - than rates of return on alternative investments of equivalent risk.

SAME-DAY SALE

The *advantages* of an ISO exercise and same-day sale of stock, relative to exercising the ISO and holding the stock for 12 months and one day, are that (1) the same-day sale *generates* cash on the date of exercise, while exercising and holding the stock *requires* cash on the date of exercise, *and* (2) the optionee eliminates the possibility of a decline in the stock price over the next 12 months.

The *disadvantages* of exercising an ISO and selling the stock on the same day is that the sale is a disqualifying disposition that triggers recognition of ordinary income, *and* it eliminates the potential for appreciation in the stock price over the next 12 months.

ANALYSIS OF THE TWO ALTERNATIVES

In order to project the future cash flows that will result *exclusively* from one alternative versus the other, the optionee first prepares three *income tax projections* for *every* tax year that will be affected by either one of the two mutually exclusive alternatives:

- Tax projection #1 assumes that No ISOs are exercised

- Tax projection #2 assumes that ISOs are exercised and the stock is sold on the same day

- Tax projection #3 assumes that ISOs are exercised and the stock is sold 12 months and one day later

All three projections assume that, 12 months and one day after the date of ISO exercise, the stock price will be equal to the exercise price. By assuming a constant stock price, the optionee isolates the cash flow effects that are associated exclusively with income taxation.

Second, the optionee prepares a schedule of the *projected future cash flows* under each alternative. That schedule shows the amount and date of each projected cash flow.

Third, using the schedule from step two, he computes the *differential cash flows* associated with one alternative relative to the other. From those differential cash flows, he computes the *projected internal rate of return (IRR)* that he earns from the decision to exercise ISOs and hold the stock for 12 months and one day.

THE ELEMENTS OF A WISE DECISION

Four sections, labeled A through D, follow this subsection:

- *Section A "Exercise ISOs and Sell the Stock on Same-Day"* shows the income tax and cash flows that result from a same-day sale of stock

- *Section B "Exercise ISOs and Sell Stock 12 Months and One Day Later"* shows the income tax and cash flows that result from holding the stock for 12 months and one day

- *Section C "Comparison of Same-Day Sale to Holding for 12 Months and One Day"* compares the cash flows from Sections A and B

- *Section D "Investment Analysis"* offers investment analysis and commentary

Sections A through D are based upon one simplified example that assumes (1) no state income taxes, (2) that exercising ISOs and holding the stock does not trigger alternative minimum tax, *and* (3) that the optionee's federal marginal income tax rate remains constant every year.

Example: Employees A and B hold ISOs on 1,000 shares of stock. The exercise price is $60 per share. The fair market value of the stock is $100 per share. The stock does not pay a dividend. Employee A's federal marginal income tax rate is 28 percent and B's is 39.6 percent. Both employees exercise options on January 15, Year 1. *Which is more advantageous - the same-day sale, or exercising and holding the stock for 12 months and one day?*

A: EXERCISE ISOs AND SELL THE STOCK ON SAME-DAY

FEDERAL INCOME TAXATION

When they exercise ISOs and sell the stock on the same day, Employees A and B make disqualifying dispositions because they do not hold the stock for more than 12 months.

Consequently, gain is taxed as *ordinary compensation* income to the extent of the *lesser* of (a) the difference between the fair market value of the stock on the date of exercise and the option price, *and* (b) the difference between the amount received in the disposition and the option price. If (b) is greater than (a), such excess is treated as a *short-term capital gain*.

For Employees A and B, (a) equals $40,000 ($100,000 - 60,000) and (b) also equals $40,000. Therefore, both recognize $40,000 of ordinary compensation income from a same-day sale. There is no short-term capital gain because (b) is *not* greater than (a).

Table 5.1 shows (1) computation of the gain, and (2) the amount of federal income tax on that gain.

CASH FLOWS

The cash flows to Employees A and B are shown in Table 5.2.

The exercise and same-day sale produces a $40,000 gain on January 15, Year 1 which is taxed as ordinary compensation income. In accordance with IRS Notice 87-49, however, the gain is *not* subject to federal income tax *withholding, not* subject to social security tax, and *not* subject to medicare tax. Consequently, the optionee receives the entire $40,000 gain on *settlement date,* generally not more than three business days after the date of sale.

Employee A incurs a federal income tax *liability* on the date of sale in the amount of $11,200 (28% X $40,000), and Employee B incurs a liability of $15,840 (39.6% X $40,000). In many situations, however, the tax is not *payable* until April 15, Year 2, the due date for filing IRS Form 1040 for the year ending December 31, Year 1.

Table 5.1

After-tax Gain for Employees A and B from a Same-Day Sale
(Assuming no State Income Tax and no AMT)

	A	B
Proceeds from sale of stock	$100,000	$100,000
Less: ISO exercise price	60,000	60,000
Pre-tax gain	40,000	40,000
Less:federal income tax[1]	11,200	15,840
After-tax gain	$ 28,800	$ 24,160

[1] Employee A's marginal income tax rate is 28% and B's is 39.6%. The $40,000 taxable gain is *not* subject to social security or medicare tax, and *not* subject to income tax *withholding*.

Table 5.2

Cash Flows to Employees A and B if Same-Day Sale
(Assuming no State Income Tax and no AMT)

Date	Event	A	B
Jan 15[3], Year 1	Exercise and sell stock[1]	$40,000	40,000
Apr 15, Year 2	Pay federal income tax[2]	- 11,200	-15,840
	Net cash flow	$28,800	24,160

[1] Proceeds from sale of stock = $100,000. Exercise price = $60,000.
[2] Employee A's marginal income tax rate is 28% and B's is 39.6%.
[3] Cash is actually received on *settlement* date, generally not more than three business days after the date of sale.

Since there is no withholding, Employees A and B have use of the entire $40,000 gain for 15 and one-half months - from January 15, Year 1 (date of sale) until April 15, Year 2 (date of tax payment).

In this example, no income tax withholding is required. In some cases, however, the optionee is required to make *estimated tax payments* as a result of gain attributable to ISOs in order to avoid a **penalty** for underpayment of estimated tax.

B. EXERCISE ISOS AND SELL STOCK 12 MONTHS AND ONE DAY LATER

In a world where individuals strive to maximize the value of ISOs, an optionee exercises ISOs well in advance of the option's expiration date because his unique needs or circumstances dictate that, at some point *between* the date of exercise and 12 months and one day later, it is time for him to sell stock. Otherwise, he would follow the general rule discussed earlier and *not* exercise until just prior to option expiration date.

Given that the optionee exercises ISOs because he has decided that it's time to sell stock, there must be an underlying incentive that would entice him to *hold* the stock. That motivating incentive - preferential tax treatment of long-term capital gains - must be strong enough to overcome the fact that if he exercises ISOs and holds the stock, he (1) incurs opportunity costs, *and* (2) assumes the risk of decline in the stock price.

OPPORTUNITY COSTS

When they exercise ISOs and make a same-day sale of stock, Employees A and B both *receive* $40,000 on settlement date (see Table 5.2). When Employees A and B exercise ISOs and *hold* the stock, they *pay* $60,000 to effect the exercise.

The *difference* between the $40,000 that they *would* receive from a same-day sale, and the $60,000 that they must *pay* to exercise and hold, is $100,000. Essentially, then, both optionees invest $100,000 (the fair market value of the stock on the date of exercise) when they exercise ISOs and hold the stock. When they invest $100,000 in the stock, this $100,000 is not available for investment elsewhere.

FEDERAL INCOME TAXATION

See Table 5.3. Recall that Employees A and B exercise ISOs on January 15, Year 1. The assumption in Table 5.3 is that they sell the stock on January 16, Year 2. The price of the stock on January 16, Year 2 (the date of sale) is $100 per share, the same as its price on January 15, Year 1 (the date of ISO exercise)

The sales by Employees A and B are *not* disqualifying dispositions because the sale date is more than 12 months after exercise date. Therefore, the $40,000 gain is taxed as long-term capital gain. Federal income tax on that gain is $8,000 for both optionees.

CASH FLOWS

The cash flows to Employees A and B are shown in Table 5.4.

On January 15, Year 1 both employees exercise ISOs by *paying* $60,000 to acquire 1,000 shares of stock. On January 16, Year 2, they both *receive* $100,000 from the sale of 1,000 shares of stock. They both realize a $40,000 long-term capital gain.

The $40,000 *long-term* capital gain is subject to income tax at the rate of 20 percent, resulting in an $8,000 federal income tax *liability*. That liability is *payable* not later than April 15, Year 3 with IRS Form 1040 for the year ending December 31, Year 2. Net cash flow from the transactions is $32,000 for both employees.

C: COMPARISON OF SAME-DAY SALE TO HOLDING FOR 12 MONTHS AND ONE DAY

The exercise and hold alternative *appears* advantageous in that the optionee pays less income tax. But, the amount of tax savings relative to the amount of money that the optionee must invest to generate that tax savings, *and* the *risk* that he takes to generate that savings might be minimal. Consequently, it is *not* always wise to exercise ISOs and hold the stock in order to receive favorable tax treatment on long-term capital gain.

TABLE 5.3

After-tax Gain from Exercising ISOs and Selling the Stock 12 Months and One Day Later in a Non-disqualifying Disposition
(Assuming no State Income Tax and no AMT)

	A	B
Sale of stock at $100 per share	$100,000	$100,000
Less: ISO exercise price	60,000	60,000
Long-term capital gain	40,000	40,000
Less: federal income tax @ 20%	8,000	8,000
After-tax gain	32,000	32,000

Table 5.4

Cash Flows to Employees A and B if They Exercise ISOs and Sell the Stock 12 Months and One Day Later
(Assuming no State Income Tax and no AMT)

Date	Event	A	B
Jan15, Year 1	Exercise ISOs on 1,000 shares[1]	-$ 60,000	- 60,000
Jan16, Year 2	Sell 1,000 shares of stock[2]	+100,000	+100,000
Apr 15, Year 3	Pay federal income tax[3]	-8,000	-8,000
Net cash flow		$ 32,000	32,000

[1] Exercise price = $60 per share.
[2] Selling price = $100 per share.
[3] Both employees pay 20 percent tax on $40,000 of long-term capital gain.

In short:

- *What is the projected rate of return on the decision to exercise and hold the stock for 12 months and one day, assuming a constant stock price?* and,

- *How does that projected rate of return compare to projected returns on alternative investments of equivalent risk?*

FEDERAL INCOME TAX

Table 5.5 compares the federal income tax liabilities that result from a same-day sale (see Table 5.1) to those that result from exercising ISOs and selling the stock 12 months and one day later (see Table 5.3).

Employees A and B both pay $8,000 in federal income tax under the exercise and hold strategy. The $8,000 tax liability is $3,200 less than Employee A pays if he makes a same-day sale. The $8,000 tax is $7,840 less than Employee B pays if he makes a same-day sale.

In other words, holding the stock for 12 months and one day is more advantageous for Employee B than for Employee A. This is because Employee B's tax rate on the $40,000 gain is reduced by 19.6 percentage points - from 39.6 percent (his marginal rate on ordinary income) to 20 percent (his tax rate on long-term capital gain). Employee A's tax rate is reduced by only 8 percentage points - from 28 percent (his marginal rate on ordinary income) to 20 percent (his tax rate on long-term capital gain).

CASH FLOWS

The cash flows from a same-day sale are presented in Table 5.2. The cash flows from exercising and holding the stock for 12 months and one day are presented in Table 5.4. The difference between the two series of cash flows for Employee A is shown in Table 5.6. The difference between the two series of cash flows for Employee B is shown in Table 5.7.

Table 5.5

**Comparison of Employee A's and B's Federal Income Tax:
Exercise ISOs and Same-Day Sale of Stock vs. Exercise ISOs
and Sell the Stock 12 Months and One Day Later
(Assuming no State Income Tax and no AMT)**

	A	B
Federal tax from a same-day sale[1]	$11,200	15,840
Federal tax from exercise and hold[2]	8,000	8,000
Federal tax savings from exercise and hold	$ 3,200	7,840

[1] from Table 5.1
[2] from Table 5.3

By analyzing the amounts and timing of the *differential* cash flows associated with these two mutually exclusive alternatives, the optionee quantifies the *projected* after-tax internal rate of return that results *exclusively* from the decision to exercise and hold. He then compares that return to expected returns on alternative investment opportunities of *equivalent risk*.

AFTER-TAX IRR

When the optionee exercises ISOs and holds the stock for 12 months and one day, he invests $100,000 for a period of 12 months and one day. He expects to earn a rate of return on that investment, a return that adequately compensates him for the risk he assumes from holding the stock.

The projected income tax savings that result from holding the stock may not be sufficient in relation to the risk that the optionee assumes of a substantial decline in the stock price. The more volatile the stock, the more risky it is to exercise ISOs and hold the stock.

Table 5.6

Differential Projected Cash Flows to Employee A, and Projected IRR from Exercising ISOs and Holding the Stock for 12 Months and One Day

DATE	(A) EXERCISE & HOLD[1]	(B) SAME-DAY SALE[2]	(A) - (B) DIFFERENCE
Jan/Yr 1	($60,000)	40,000	($100,000)
Jan/Yr 2	100,000	0	100,000
Apr/Yr 2	0	(11,200)	11,200
Apr/Yr 3	(8,000)	0	(8,000)
Net cash flow	32,000	28,800	3,200

Projected after-tax IRR from the decision to <u>exercise and hold</u>:

Projected after-tax annual IRR = 3.4% (compounded monthly)

[1] from Table 5.4
[2] from Table 5.2

Table 5.8 shows the projected *after-tax annual internal rate of return (IRR)*, compounded monthly, that results *exclusively* from the decision to exercise ISOs and sell the stock 12 months and one day later, as opposed to making an exercise and same-day sale. The returns shown in this table assume a constant stock price, a constant federal marginal income tax rate, no state income tax, no alternative minimum tax, and various other factors as disclosed in the table.

Notice from Table 5.8 that, all things being equal, the higher the federal marginal income tax rate on ordinary income, the higher the projected after-tax return from exercising and holding, relative to the same-day sale. Also notice that, all things being equal, the lower the exercise price of the ISO relative to the stock price on the date of exercise, the higher the projected after-tax return from exercising and holding.

Table 5.7

Differential Projected Cash Flows to Employee B, and Projected IRR from Exercising ISOs and Holding the Stock for 12 Months and One Day

DATE	(A) EXERCISE & HOLD[1]	(B) SAME-DAY SALE[2]	(A) - (B) DIFFERENCE
Jan/Yr 1	($60,000)	40,000	($100,000)
Jan/Yr 2	100,000	0	100,000
Apr/Yr 2	0	(15,840)	15,840
Apr/Yr 3	(8,000)	0	(8,000)
Net cash flow	32,000	24,160	7,840

Projected after-tax IRR from the decision to <u>exercise and hold</u>:

Projected after-tax annual IRR = 8.0% (compounded monthly)

[1] from Table 5.4
[2] from Table 5.2

The exercise and hold strategy becomes increasingly attractive when the optionee's marginal tax rate on ordinary income is higher or when his gain is larger, or both. This is logical because under these two conditions the optionee enjoys more of an income tax savings from converting ordinary income into long-term capital gain.

Since many variables affect the IRR, and since the assumptions used in Table 5.8 are unlikely to fit exactly the unique circumstances of individual optionees, Table 5.8 should be used as a guide only. It is not a substitute for comprehensive planning, particularly when large sums of money are involved.

Example: Debra holds ISOs that have an exercise price equal to 30 percent of the current stock price. Her income is subject to a federal marginal income tax rate of 39.6 percent. Table 5.8 shows that Debra earns an after-tax return of 14.1 percent if she exercises the options and holds the stock for 12 months and one day, relative to exercising options and making a same-day sale of stock.

Comprehensive planning, however, shows a projected after-tax return of only 9.7 percent on the decision to exercise and hold. The following factors affect Debra's projected return. First, her income *is* subject to state income taxation. Second, the AMT *does* impact her projected cash flows. Third, she exercises ISOs on August 15, not January 15.

Table 5.8

Projected After-tax Annual Rate of Return from the Decision to Exercise ISOs and Sell the Stock 12 Months and One Day Later

EXERCISE PRICE AS A % OF STOCK PRICE	MARGINAL INCOME TAX RATE			
	28%	31%	36%	39.6%
90%	.8%	1.1	1.6	2.0
80	1.6	2.3	3.3	4.0
70	2.5	3.4	4.9	6.0
60	**3.4**	4.6	6.6	**8.0**
50	4.3	5.8	8.3	10.0
40	5.2	7.1	10.0	12.0
30	6.2	8.3	11.7	**14.1**
20	7.1	9.6	13.5	16.1
10	8.1	10.9	15.2	18.1

Assumptions:

1. Employee exercises ISO on January 15
2. ISO exercise does not trigger alternative minimum tax
3. Excluding the impact of state income taxes and transaction costs
4. Neither alternative affects estimated tax payment requirements
5. The stock does not pay a dividend
6. Optionee's marginal income tax rate is the same every year
7. Tax rate on long-term capital gains is 20 percent

D: INVESTMENT ANALYSIS

Which alternative is more attractive - exercise ISOs and hold the stock for 12 months and one day, or exercise ISOs and sell the stock on the same day? For some optionees, there *isn't* a choice. They don't have the financial resources to exercise the option *and hold* the stock. Consequently, they make a cashless exercise followed by an immediate sale of stock.

For others, it depends. The projected IRR associated with exercising and holding may, or may not, be high enough to justify the risk associated with holding the stock for 12 months and one day.

EMPLOYEE A

Employee A's exercise price ($60 per share) as a percentage of the stock price ($100 per share) on the date of exercise is 60 percent. His marginal income tax rate is 28 percent.

The decision to exercise ISOs and sell the stock 12 months and one day later generates a *projected after-tax* annual rate of return of 3.4 percent (see Table 5.8). This return is equivalent to a *pre-tax* return of 4.72 percent for Employee A who is subject to income tax at the rate of 28 percent (3.4 percent/(1-.28)).

Employee A realizes that this 4.72 percent return is even *less* than he could earn on default-free, one-year U.S. Treasury Bills. Dissatisfied that the 4.72 percent projected return does not adequately compensate him for the uncertainty surrounding the price of his employer's stock at the end of 12 months and one day, he wisely decides that it doesn't make sense to exercise and hold.

EMPLOYEE B

Employee B's exercise price as a percentage of the stock price on the date of exercise is also 60 percent. His marginal income tax rate is 39.6 percent (11.6 percentage points higher than Employee A's marginal rate).

The decision to exercise ISOs and sell the stock 12 months and one day later generates a *projected after-tax* annual rate of return of 8.0 percent (see Table 5.8). This return is equivalent to a *pre-tax* return of 13.24 percent for Employee B who is subject to income tax at the rate of 39.6 percent (8.0 percent/(1-.396)).

Employee B invests the *same* amount of money and assumes the *same* risk as Employee A when both exercise ISOs and hold the stock for 12 months and one day. But, Employee B's projected rate of return is substantially higher. His projected return is higher because Employee B enjoys more of an income tax savings (a savings of $7,840 for B and only $3,200 for A – see Table 5.5) when he converts ordinary income into long-term capital gain.

Employee B, like Employee A, compares the projected 8.0 percent after-tax return to expected returns on alternative investments of equivalent risk before deciding to exercise ISOs and hold the stock for 12 months and one day.

CONCLUSION

If he exercises ISOs and holds the stock for 12 months and one day, the optionee invests an amount of money that is equal to the fair market value of the optioned stock on the date of exercise. For example, if he holds ISOs on 1,000 shares of stock and the fair market value of that stock is $100 per share on the date of option exercise, he invests $100,000 (1,000 shares X $100 per share) on the date of option exercise.

Naturally, the risk associated with the investment depends upon the volatility of the stock price. Other things being equal, the less volatile the stock, the more attractive it is to exercise ISOs and hold the stock.

The projected rate of return that results *exclusively* from the decision to exercise ISOs and hold the stock for 12 months and one day is different for each optionee. It is a function of several factors, including, (1) the price of the stock at the end of 12 months and one day, (2) the employee's marginal income tax rate on ordinary income, (3) the income tax rate on long term capital gains, (4) the relationship between the exercise price of the option and the stock price on the date of exercise, (5) whether, or to what extent, the alternative minimum tax impacts the amounts and timing of cash flows, (6) the date of exercise, (7) dividend yield on the stock, *and* (8) whether, or to what extent, either of the two mutually exclusive alternatives affects the amounts and timing of estimated tax payments.

As a general rule, exercise and hold is almost *never* a wise decision for the optionee who is subject to a marginal income tax rate of 28 percent or lower, it is *rarely* wise for the optionee who is subject to a 31 percent marginal rate, and it is *sometimes* wise for optionees who are subject to marginal rates of 36 percent or higher.

For many optionees, exercising ISOs and selling the stock 12 months and one day later, in order to receive preferential tax treatment, is not the panacea that it is sometimes thought to be.

MODIFYING THE RISK OF HOLDING THE STOCK

When he exercises an ISO and holds the stock for 12 months and one day, the optionee assumes the risk that the value of the stock that he holds will decline.

The relevant question then becomes: "How can the appreciation in the stock price be protected *and* the optionee still receive preferential tax treatment on long-term capital gain?" The optionee could *attempt* to achieve this desired result by purchasing put options (at the time he exercises the ISO) on some *other* security or basket of other securities whose fair market value can be expected to move in tandem with the fair market value of the stock he acquires by option exercise.

Put options have a tendency to increase in value when the price of the underlying security declines. The *hope* is that if the price of his stock declines, appreciation in the fair market value of the put options will offset most or all of that decline.

This strategy comes with a cost, and a risk. The *cost* is the price of the option. The *risk* is that the price of his stock declines and the underlying security or basket of securities does *not* decline or declines by a lesser amount. If this happens, gain, if any, on the put options will be insufficient to offset the decline in the value of the optionee's stock.

II. EARLY EXERCISE

Optionees that hold nonqualified stock options sometimes exercise them *early* with the intention of *holding* the stock for more than 12 months, and often for a much *longer* period.

They do this with the *expectation* that they will convert *anticipated future appreciation* in the stock price after the date of option exercise, from ordinary income into more favorably taxed long-term capital gain. If they hold the stock for more than 12 months after the date of option exercise, 100 percent of any appreciation in the stock price that occurs *after the date of exercise* is taxed as long-term capital gain.

This strategy comes with risk. It produces inferior returns relative to other investment alternatives when the stock price does *not* appreciate sufficiently. The price of the stock may even decline subsequent to the option exercise.

Obviously, the less risky alternative is to exercise the option *after,* and *if,* anticipated appreciation in the stock price materializes. The *disadvantage*, however, is that this less risky strategy comes with less favorable income tax treatment. One hundred percent of the excess of the fair market value of the stock on the [eventual] exercise date over the exercise price is taxed as *ordinary* income on the date of exercise.

CONVERTING ORDINARY INCOME INTO CAPITAL GAIN

In most cases, the *exercise* of a NQSO triggers the recognition of *ordinary compensation income* in the amount of the excess, if any, of the fair market value of the stock at the time of exercise over the exercise price.

Table 5.9 shows that the optionee recognizes *no* taxable income if he exercises the option on the date that it is granted *and* the fair market value of the stock is equal to the option's exercise price (which is usually the case). His *basis* in the stock acquired is $100, its fair market value on the date of option exercise.

Table 5.9

Exercise NQSO on Grant Date (Year 1)

Fair market value of stock	$ 100[1]
Less: exercise price	100
Ordinary compensation income	None

[1] the optionee's basis in the stock is $100, the stock's fair market value on date of option exercise

Table 5.10 shows that if he sells the stock in Year 6 for $500, he recognizes $400 of long-term capital gain.

Table 5.10

Sale of Stock Previously Acquired by Exercise of NQSO (Year 6)

Proceeds from sale of stock	$ 500
Less: fair market value on date of option exercise	100
Long-term capital gain	$ 400

If the optionee would have *waited* until Year 6 to exercise the NQSO (instead of exercising the option in Year 1) and sell the stock, he would *not* have received preferential income tax treatment on long-term capital gain.

The *intended* result of the "exercise early" strategy is that the optionee holds the stock for more than 12 months, its price increases substantially after the date of option exercise, and he pays income tax at the lower tax rate on *long-term capital gains.* By exercising early, he converts 100 percent of the appreciation in the stock price that occurs after the option's exercise date, from ordinary income into long-term capital gain.

IS IT WISE TO EXERCISE A NQSO EARLY?

Whether or not early exercise makes sense depends upon a number of factors, the most important being the future rate of appreciation in the price of the stock. The more rapid the appreciation, the more likely that an early exercise is more advantageous than holding the NQSO and waiting to exercise (other things being equal).

In theory, it is possible to project the *minimum* rate of appreciation in the price of the stock, after the date of option exercise, that makes an early exercise attractive. That rate of appreciation is dependent upon a number of factors, including - the exercise price, the stock price, the optionee's marginal income tax rate on ordinary income, the tax rate on long-term capital gains, dividend yield on the stock, and interest rates. Tables 5.11 and 5.12 illustrate this point.

In Table 5.11 the optionee exercises the NQSO on grant date when the fair market value of the stock *equals* the exercise price of the option. Consequently, he does not recognize any taxable income on the date of exercise (because the fair market value of the stock on the date of exercise does not exceed the exercise price). He recognizes long-term capital gain in Year 6, the year that he sells the stock.

The example shown in Table 5.11 incorporates the following assumptions: (1) the optionee exercises the NQSO in Year 1 at an exercise price of $100 when the fair market value of the stock is $100, (2) long-term capital gains in Year 6 are taxed at 20 percent, (3) the stock price appreciates at an annual rate of 16 percent, from $100 in Year 1 to $210 in Year 6, *and* (5) the stock does not pay a dividend.

In summary, the optionee invests $100 in Year 1. The after-tax terminal value in Year 6 is $188.

In Table 5.12 the optionee does *not* exercise early. He waits until Year 6 to exercise the NQSO and recognizes *ordinary* income in the amount of the excess of the fair market value of the stock on the date of exercise over the exercise price. He sells the stock *immediately* after option exercise and therefore does not realize any capital gain or loss because the fair market value of the stock on the date of sale is exactly equal to his basis (fair market value on the date of exercise).

The example shown in Table 5.12 incorporates the following assumptions: (1) as an alternative to paying $100 to exercise the NQSO in Year 1, the optionee uses that $100 to buy U.S. Series EE savings bonds in Year 1 and redeems them in Year 6, (2) the savings bonds yield 6.225 percent compounded annually, (3) the optionee exercises the NQSO in Year 6, at an exercise price of $100, and immediately sells the stock, (4) the stock price appreciates at an annual rate of 16 percent, from $100 in Year 1 to $210 in Year 6, *and* (5) the optionee's federal marginal income tax rate in Year 6 is 39.6 percent.

Table 5.11

Exercise NQSO in Year 1
Sell the Stock in Year 6
Terminal Value of the Investment
(Assuming no State Income Tax)

Year⇒	1	2	3	4	5	6
Exercise NQSO	($100)					
Tax on NQSO exercise	0^1					
Sell stock						210
Income tax on LTCG						$(22)^2$
Net cash flow	($100)	0	0	0	0	188

[1] income tax on exercise date is zero since the $100 stock price equals the $100 exercise price
[2] payable not later than April 15, Year 7 with IRS Form 1040

In summary, the optionee invests $100 in Year 1. The after-tax terminal value at the end of Year 6 is $188.

CONCLUSION

Under the assumptions presented in Tables 5.11 and 5.12, the after-tax terminal values are equal ($188). The optionee would be *indifferent* to exercising early versus waiting to exercise the NQSO.

The answer to the question *"Exercise early or not?"* is highly dependent upon future appreciation of the stock price. If the assumptions in Table 5.11 and 5.12 are changed such that the stock price appreciates at an annual rate of more than 16 percent, the early exercise provides a higher terminal value. At rates of appreciation less than 16 percent, the early exercise results in a lower terminal value.

Table 5.12

**Purchase U.S. Series EE Savings Bonds in Year 1
Exercise NQSO in Year 6. Sell the Stock in Year 6
Terminal Value of the Investment
(Assuming no State Income Tax)**

Year⇒	1	2	3	4	5	6
Purchase bonds[1]	($100)					
Redeem bonds[1]						136
Tax on interest income						$(14)^2$
Exercise NQSO						(100)
Sell stock						210
Tax on NQSO exercise						$(44)^3$
Net cash flow	($100)					$188

[1] U.S. Series EE savings bonds
[2] tax on savings bonds interest income = 39.6% x ($136 - 100) = $14; payable not later than April 15, Year 7 with IRS Form 1040
[3] 39.6% x ($210 - 100) = $44; payable not later than April 15, Year 7 with IRS Form 1040

The alternatives illustrated in Tables 5.11 and 5.12 resulted in the *same* terminal values at the end of five years ($188). The early exercise, however, involved substantially more risk. Consequently, its *risk-adjusted* return is lower than the wait-to-exercise alternative.

As discussed earlier, it is theoretically possible to determine the minimum rate of appreciation in the stock price that must occur after the date of option exercise, in order for the exercise early alternative to *appear* attractive. The following section shows that such appearances can be misleading…and *costly*. It illustrates that an outright purchase of the stock, while continuing to hold the option, is preferable to early exercise of the option.

RETAINING THE NQSO AND BUYING THE STOCK OUTRIGHT

If the expectation is that the stock price will appreciate substantially, it naturally follows that *retaining* the nonqualified stock option, and buying the stock outright, is usually preferable to buying the stock by exercising the option. This strategy allows the optionee to retain the advantages of holding the option while reaping any benefits than stem from owning the stock.

See Table 5.13. The example in Table 5.13 assumes (1) that the optionee's federal marginal income tax rate is 39.6 percent, (2) an option exercise price of $80 per share, *and* (3) a current stock price of $100 per share.

Alternative A is to purchase one share of stock at $100 and *retain* the NQSO to purchase one share at $80. Alternative A requires a total investment of $100.

Alternative B is to *exercise* the NQSO by paying $80 to purchase one share of stock that has a fair market value of $100. The $20 excess of the fair market value of the stock on the date of exercise over the exercise price is taxed as ordinary compensation income, at a marginal income tax rate of 39.6 percent. The income tax liability on that $20 gain is $8. Alternative B requires a total investment of $88.

Clearly, Alternative A is preferable to B. When he selects Alternative A, the optionee effectively pays $12 (see Table 5.13 "Alt A-B") to retain an option that has an *intrinsic value* of $20 (the $100 fair market value of the stock minus the $80 exercise price of the option) and a *fair market value* that may be worth substantially more than $20, depending upon a number of factors, including the amount of time remaining until the option's expiration date. The more time remaining, the more valuable the option.

Table 5.14 clearly illustrates that when the optionee exercises early he literally discards his option. He throws it into the waste receptacle.

In Table 5.14, the optionee holds an option to purchase one share of stock at an exercise price of $100. The fair market value of the stock is $100.

If he pays $100 to buy the stock outright (and retains the option), he holds one share of stock *and* an option to buy one share of stock at $100. This scenario is identified in Table 5.14 as Alternative A.

Table 5.13
Retaining the NQSO and Buying the Stock (Alternative A) versus Exercising the NQSO (Alternative B)

Alt A	Buy 1 share @ $100 per share	$100
	Retain option to purchase 1 share @ $80	0
	Total investment Alternative A	$100
Alt B	Exercise:buy 1 share @ $80 per share	80
	Income tax @ 39.6% on $20 gain	8
	Total investment Alternative B	$ 88
Alt A-B	*Difference in amount of investment*	$ 12

Instead, if he exercises the option, he pays the $100 exercise price and he holds one share of stock. *But* his option is gone. This scenario is identified in Table 5.14 as Alternative B.

Clearly, Alternative A is preferable to B. See "Alt A-B" in Table 5.14 which illustrates that the optionee effectively pays *nothing* to retain the option when he chooses Alternative A.

Table 5.14

Retaining the NQSO and Buying the Stock (Alternative A) versus Exercising the NQSO (Alternative B)

Alt A	Buy 1 share @ $100 per share	$100
	Retain option to purchase 1 share @ $100	0
	Total investment Alternative A	$100
Alt B	Exercise:buy 1 share @ $100 per share	100
	Income tax @ 39.6% on $0 gain	0
	Total investment Alternative B	$100
Alt A-B	*Difference in amount of investment*	$ 0

Stated another way, when he exercises the option early, he sacrifices the option. The option that he sacrifices has value, a value which could be substantial depending upon a number of factors including the volatility of the stock and the amount of time remaining until the option's expiration date.

ISOs: EXERCISE EARLY AND HOLD THE STOCK

In most situations, optionees that hold ISOs should *not* exercise options with the intention of holding the stock for *more than* 12 months and one day. Once they have held the stock for 12 months and one day, 100 percent of the gain on the date of sale is taxed as long-term capital gain. There is *no* income tax advantage to holding the stock for *more than* 12 months and one day.

6

IRS Form 1040 Reporting

NONQUALIFIED STOCK OPTIONS

GRANT DATE

The optionee does *not* report to the Internal Revenue Service the fact that a corporation granted him a nonqualified stock option.

TAX REPORTING FOR THE YEAR OF EXERCISE

The exercise of a nonqualified stock option results in the recognition of ordinary compensation income in the amount of the excess, if any, of the fair market value of the stock on the date of exercise over the exercise price.

- The corporation reports the income as *wages* on the optionee's IRS Form W-2 *"Wage and Tax Statement" regardless* if the optionee sells the stock that he acquires by exercising the option. The optionee reports those wages on page 1 of IRS Form 1040.

- If the income is *not* reported to the optionee as wages on IRS Form W-2, the optionee should report the income as *"Other Income"* on IRS Form 1040, page 1 accompanied by the description *"Exercise of nonqualified stock option(s) to purchase stock in [name of corporation]"*.

TAX REPORTING FOR THE YEAR OF SALE

Every sale of stock must be reported on IRS Form 1040, Schedule D *"Capital Gains and Losses"*. This statement is true regardless if the sale results in a capital gain, a capital loss, or no capital gain or loss.

In most cases, the optionee recognizes a *capital gain or loss* on the date of sale, even when he sells the stock on the same date that he exercises the option, because stock prices sometimes fluctuate from one minute to the next.

- The optionee reports the sale of stock on IRS Form 1040, Schedule D.

- If the date of sale is more than 12 months after the date of option exercise, gain or loss is taxed as long-term capital gain or loss. If the stock is not held for more than 12 months, gain or loss is taxed as short-term capital gain or loss.

INCENTIVE STOCK OPTIONS

GRANT DATE

The optionee does *not* report to the Internal Revenue Service the fact that he has been granted an incentive stock option.

TAX REPORTING FOR THE YEAR OF EXERCISE

An ISO exercise results in taxable income for alternative minimum tax purposes in the amount of the excess of the fair market value of the stock on the date of exercise over the exercise price - *whether or not* the stock is sold during the calendar year of exercise.

- If the stock is *not* sold during the calendar year in which the option is exercised, the optionee reports the income in Part I of IRS Form 6251 *"Alternative Minimum Tax - Individuals"* for the tax year in which the exercise occurs.

- If the stock *is* sold in the calendar year of exercise, the optionee does *not* report the income on IRS Form 6251 - although it *is* subject to AMT tax - because the income is already included in the optionee's computation of regular taxable income.

TAX REPORTING FOR THE YEAR OF SALE

As discussed earlier with respect to nonqualified stock options, *every* sale of stock previously acquired by exercise of an incentive stock option must be reported on IRS Form 1040, Schedule D *"Capital Gains and Losses"* for the tax year in which the stock is sold. For example, the optionee reports a sale of stock that occurs on December 5, 1998 on his 1998 income tax return.

NON-DISQUALIFYING DISPOSITIONS

- The optionee reports the sale of stock on IRS Form 1040, Schedule D. The difference between the sales proceeds and the exercise price (his basis in the stock) is taxed as *long-term* capital gain or loss.

- The optionee recognizes less income for purposes of AMT than he does for purposes of the regular tax. In order to avoid the potential for overpayment of AMT in the year of sale, the optionee reports (as a *negative* amount) for the year of sale, the excess of what the fair market value of the stock was on the date of ISO exercise over the exercise price as *"Adjusted gain or loss"* in Part I of IRS Form 6251.

DISQUALIFYING DISPOSITIONS

If the optionee sells the stock in the <u>same</u> calendar year that he exercises the ISO:

- *If proceeds from the sale are less than the ISO exercise price:*

    - The optionee does not recognize any ordinary compensation income. He reports the sale of stock on IRS Form 1040, Schedule D. The sale results in a *short-term* capital *loss* in the amount of the difference between the sales proceeds and the exercise price (his basis in the stock).

- *If proceeds from the sale are greater than or equal to what the fair market value was on the date of ISO exercise:*

    - The employer reports *wages* to the optionee on IRS Form W-2 in the amount of the excess of the fair market value of the stock on the date of exercise over the exercise price. The optionee reports these wages on IRS Form 1040, page 1.

    - If the income is *not* reported to the optionee as wages on IRS Form W-2, the optionee should report the excess of the fair market value of the stock on the date of exercise over the exercise price as *"Other Income"* on IRS Form 1040, page 1 accompanied by the description *"Disqualifying disposition of [name of corporation] stock"*.

    - The optionee reports the sale of stock on IRS Form 1040, Schedule D. The excess of the sales proceeds over the fair market value of the stock on the date of exercise (his basis in the stock) is taxed as *short-term* capital gain.

- *If proceeds from the sale are greater than the exercise price but less than what the fair market value was on the date of ISO exercise*:

  - The employer reports *wages* to the optionee on IRS Form W-2 in the amount of the excess of the proceeds from the sale over the exercise price. The optionee reports these wages on IRS Form 1040, page 1.

  - If the income is *not* reported to the optionee as wages on IRS Form W-2, the optionee should report the excess of the proceeds from the sale over the exercise price as *"Other Income"* on IRS Form 1040, page 1 accompanied by the description *"Disqualifying disposition of [name of corporation] stock"*.

  - The optionee reports the sale of stock as a short-term capital gain or loss on IRS Form 1040, Schedule D. The amount of the gain or loss is equal to the difference between the sales proceeds and the optionee's basis in the stock. His basis in the stock is equal to the sum of the exercise price *plus* the amount of ordinary compensation income (wages) that he recognizes (which is generally reported to him on IRS Form W-2) as a result of the disqualifying disposition.

If the optionee sells the stock in the year <u>following</u> the calendar year that he exercises the ISO:

- *If proceeds from the sale are less than the ISO exercise price*:

  - The optionee does not recognize any ordinary compensation income. He reports the sale of stock on IRS Form 1040, Schedule D. The sale results in a *capital loss* in the amount of the difference between the sales proceeds and the exercise price (his basis in the stock). If the stock is not held for more than 12 months (which is most often the case in a disqualifying disposition), the loss is taxed as a short-term capital loss. If the date of sale is more than 12 months after the date of option exercise, the loss is taxed as a long-term capital gain or loss.

The optionee also reports (as a *negative* amount), the excess of the fair market value of the stock on the date of ISO exercise over the exercise price as *"Adjusted gain or loss"* in Part I of IRS Form 6251. This second entry ensures that he does not overpay AMT in the year of sale.

- *If proceeds from the sale are greater than or equal to what the fair market value was on the date of ISO exercise*

    The employer reports *wages* to the optionee on IRS Form W-2 in the amount of the excess of the fair market value of the stock on the date of exercise over the exercise price. The optionee reports these wages on IRS Form 1040, page 1.

    If the income is *not* reported to the optionee as wages on IRS Form W-2, the optionee should report the excess of the fair market value of the stock on the date of exercise over the exercise price as *"Other Income"* on IRS Form 1040, page 1 accompanied by the description *"Disqualifying disposition of [name of corporation] stock"*.

    The optionee reports the sale of stock on IRS Form 1040, Schedule D. The excess of the proceeds from the sale over the fair market value of the stock on the date of exercise (his basis in the stock) is taxed as capital gain, short or long-term depending if the date of sale is more than 12 months after the date of ISO exercise.

    The optionee also reports (as a *negative* amount), the excess of the fair market value of the stock on the date of ISO exercise over the exercise price as *"Adjusted gain or loss"* in Part I of IRS Form 6251. This second entry ensures that he does not overpay AMT in the year of sale.

- *If proceeds from the sale are greater than the exercise price but less than what the fair market value was on the date of ISO exercise*:

> The employer reports *wages* to the optionee on IRS Form W-2 in the amount of the excess of the proceeds from the sale over the exercise price. The optionee reports these wages on IRS Form 1040, page 1.

> If the income is *not* reported to the optionee as wages on IRS Form W-2, the optionee should report the excess of the proceeds from the sale over the exercise price as *"Other Income"* on IRS Form 1040, page 1 accompanied by the description *"Disqualifying disposition of [name of corporation] stock"*.

> The optionee reports the sale of stock on IRS Form 1040, Schedule D. The amount of the capital gain or loss is equal to the difference between the sales proceeds and the optionee's basis in the stock. His basis in the stock is equal to the sum of the exercise price *plus* the amount of ordinary compensation income (wages) that he recognizes (which is generally reported to him on IRS Form W-2) as a result of the disqualifying disposition. If the date of sale is more than 12 months after the date of ISO exercise, the gain or loss is taxed as long-term capital gain or loss. In most cases, however, the date of sale is not more than 12 months after the date of ISO exercise in which case the gain or loss is taxed as short-term capital gain or loss.

> The optionee also reports (as a *negative* amount), the excess of the fair market value of the stock on the date of ISO exercise over the exercise price as *"Adjusted gain or loss"* in Part I of IRS Form 6251. This second

entry ensures that he does not overpay AMT in the year of sale.

Appendix_____

Tax Research

- PRIVATE LETTER RULING 9629028

- REVENUE RULING 80-244

- IRS NOTICE 87-49

- REGULATION 1.83-2

- REGULATION 1.83-3(j)

- REGULATION 1.83-7

PRIVATE LETTER RULING 9629028

PLR 9629028, 07/19/96 -- IRC Secs. 422, 421, 424, 1036, 1012, 1031, 1223, 83
July 19, 1996
Code secs. 422; 421; 424; 1036; 1012; 1031; 1223; 83
Uil nos.   0083.11-00; 0421.02-00
Incentive and nonqualified stock options--payment--previously acquired stock--certification--constructive delivery.
Headnote

Incentive and nonqualified stock option plan sponsor's certification procedure, which allowed optionees to use previously acquired shares to pay option exercise price without physically delivering those "payment shares" to corp., constituted constructive delivery of the payment shares for federal tax purposes. So, payment shares that were acquired by previous exercise of ISO and that met Code Sec. 422 holding requirements, or by NQSO or on the open market, to pay for ISO, would be treated as if optionee physically surrendered those shares for Code Sec. 421Code Sec. 422Code Sec. 424Code Sec. 1036Code Sec. 1012Code Sec. 1031Code Sec. 1223 purposes; and similar treatment applied to use of payment shares that hadn't met the holding requirements to pay for ISO, and to constructive payment of NQSO. Also, ISO wasn't "modified" under Code Sec. 424(h) ; and corp. didn't have to amend its plans before instituting the procedure.
References: Code Sec. 83Code Sec. 421Code Sec. 422Code Sec. 424Code Sec. 1012Code Sec. 1031Code Sec. 1036Code Sec. 1223
Full Text
Date: April 24, 1996
TR-31-2741-95/CC:EBEO:4
LEGEND:

Company = * * *
Dear * * *
This is in response to a letter dated December 5, 1995, submitted on behalf of the Company, requesting rulings concerning

certain stock option plans maintained by the Company and certain of its subsidiaries.

The Company is a corporation that currently maintains three stock option plans (collectively referred to as the "Plans"). Options granted under the Plans may be either incentive stock options ("ISOs") or nonqualified stock options ("NQSOs"). No option granted under the Plans is assignable or transferrable, except by will or the laws of descent and distribution. No option granted under the Plans is exercisable during an option holder's lifetime except by the option holder.

The Plans expressly provide that options may be exercised, in whole or in part, by the surrender (or delivery) to the Company of previously acquired shares of its common stock. The Company, through the Compensation Committee of its Board of Directors, has officially interpreted the Plans to allow employees to exercise options granted under the Plans by constructively surrendering previously acquired Company stock in payment for the shares to be received under the option exercise. Consistent with this interpretation, the Company proposes to allow employees, in connection with the exercise of an option that permits payment with shares of Company stock, to make a constructive exchange of Company shares already owned ("Payment Shares"), in lieu of actually tendering such Company stock to the Company. If the Payment Shares are held by a registered securities broker for the optionee in "street name," the optionee would provide the Company with a notarized statement attesting to the number of shares owned that are intended to serve as Payment Shares. If the Company stock certificates are actually held by the optionee, he would provide the Company with their certificate numbers. Upon receipt of a notarized statement regarding ownership of the Payment Shares, or upon confirmation of ownership of the Payment Shares by reference to Company records, the Company would treat the Payment Shares as being constructively exchanged, and therefore issue to the employee a certificate for a net number of shares: the number of shares subject to the option exercise less the number of Payment Shares.

Section 83(a) of the Internal Revenue Code generally provides that if, in connection with the performance of services, property is transferred to any person other than the person for whom the services were performed, the excess of the fair market value of the property over the amount paid for the property is included in the service provider's gross income in the first taxable year in which the rights of the service provider in the property are transferable or are not subject to a substantial risk of forfeiture.

Pursuant to section 83(e) of the Code and section 1.83- 7(a) of the Income Tax Regulations, an individual only recognizes income under section 83(a), with respect to an option that does not have a readily ascertainable fair market value, upon the transfer of stock at the time the option is exercised.

Section 1.83-7(b) of the regulations provides that an option does not have a readily ascertainable fair market value if it is not traded on an established market and it is not transferable.

Section 421(a) of the Code provides that, if an individual receives stock by exercising an ISO and the requirements of Section 422(a) are met, the individual will not recognize any income at the time of the transfer.

Section 421(b) of the Code provides that a "disqualifying disposition" occurs when an individual "disposes" of stock received pursuant to an ISO before meeting the holding period requirements of section 422(a) and that the disposition results in the individual's recognizing compensation income attributable to the disposition.

Section 1.422A-1(b)(3), Example (3) of the proposed regulations states that, upon a disqualifying disposition, an individual recognizes as ordinary income the difference between the exercise price of the option and the fair market value of the acquired stock when the option was exercised and recognizes as capital gain the difference between the fair market value of the acquired stock when the option was exercised and the amount realized upon the disqualifying disposition.

To satisfy the holding period requirements of section 422(a) of the Code, an optionee cannot dispose of stock received pursuant to an ISO within the two-year period after the ISO is granted or within the one-year period following the date the stock is transferred to the optionee.

Section 422(c)(4) of the Code provides that an employee may pay for stock pursuant to an ISO with stock of the corporation granting the option.

Section 1.422A-2(i)(1)(iii)(A) and (B) of the proposed regulations state, in part, that, if an individual exercises an ISO solely with previously acquired stock and section 1036(a) of the Code applies, the individual's basis in the acquired shares, up to the-number of exchanged shares, will be equal to the individual's bases in the exchanged shares, and, except for purposes of section 422(a)(1), the holding period of such stock will be determined under section 1223, whereas the individual's basis in acquired shares exceeding the number of exchanged shares will be zero, and the holding period of such stock will begin on the date of the transfer.

Section 424(c)(1) of the Code defines a disposition for purposes of sections 421-424 as a "sale, exchange, gift, or transfer of legal title." Section 424(c)(1)(B) excludes from this definition a stock for stock exchange to which section 1036(a) applies.

Section 424(c)(3) of the Code provides that the nonrecognition rules of Section 1036(a) do not apply to a transfer" of stock that was previously acquired through the exercise of an ISO in connection with the exercise of any ISO if the previously acquired stock has not met the holding period requirements of section 422(a)(1).

Section 424(h) of the Code provides that a 'modification' of the terms of an ISO is considered the granting of a new option and defines 'modification' as any change in the terms of an ISO that gives the employee additional benefits under the ISO.

Section 1.425-1(e)(5)(i) of the proposed regulations explains that a modification includes a change that provides more favorable terms for payment for the stock purchased under the ISO, such as the right to tender previously acquired stock.

Section 1012 of the Code provides that property has a basis equal to its cost.

Section 1031(d) of the Code provides that the basis of stock received in a stock for stock exchange to which section 1036(a) applies is the same as the basis of the stock exchanged.

Section 1036(a) of the Code provides that no gain or loss is recognized when common stock of a corporation is exchanged for common stock of that same corporation.

Section 1223(1) of the Code provides that the capital asset holding period of stock acquired in exchange for stock includes the period for which the exchanged stock was held, if the acquired stock has the same basis as the exchanged stock.

Rev. Rul. 80-244, 1980-2 C.B. 234, concludes that, when stock acquired pursuant to the exercise of a qualified stock option is used (to the extent of its fair market value) to pay the full exercise price of a nonqualified stock option at a point in time when the stock acquired pursuant to the exercise of the qualified option had not met the holding period requirements, (i) the basis in the shares of stock received on the exercise of the nonqualified stock option that are equal in number to the shares of stock used as payment is the same as the basis in the stock used as payment, (ii) a 'disposition' of the stock acquired pursuant to the exercise of the qualified options does not occur and (iii) the fair market value of any additional shares received will be includible in income as compensation. The adjusted basis of those shares would then be the amount included in income. Also see, section 1.422A-2(i)(4), example 4, of the proposed regulations.

In this case, an option holder will be permitted to pay the option exercise price by a certification procedure that eliminates the need to physically deliver previously acquired shares to the Company. Under the certification procedure, an option holder will provide the Company with either a notarized statement attesting to the number of shares owned that are intended as Payment Shares, or the certificate numbers of the Payment Shares.

Based upon the information submitted, we conclude that the Company's certification procedure, which eliminates the need to physically deliver Payment Shares to the Company, will be deemed a constructive delivery of such shares for Federal income tax purposes, and accordingly provide the following rulings:

(1) An optionee who constructively pays the exercise price of an ISO with Payment Shares that (i) were previously acquired through the exercise of an ISO and that have satisfied the holding requirements of Section 422(a) of the Code ("Mature ISO Stock") or (ii) that were acquired by some other means such as through the exercise of an NQSO ("NQSO Stock") or purchased on the open market would receive the same tax treatment as if the optionee had physically surrendered shares that had satisfied the holding period, if applicable,

specifically:

(a) The optionee will not recognize income upon the exercise of the ISO. Sections 421(a)(1), 422(c)(4)(A), 424(c)(1)(B) 424(c)(3). Furthermore, the optionee will not recognize capital gain or loss on the constructive surrender of previously owned shares. See section 1036(a).

(b) The optionee will have a carryover basis with respect to those shares of stock deemed to be received that are equal in number to the Payment Shares. The basis in any stock actually received will be the cash, if any, paid on the transfer. Sections 1012, and 1031(d).

(c) For purposes of section 1223(1), the optionee will have a carryover holding period with respect to those shares of stock deemed to be received that are equal in number to the Payment Shares, whereas the holding period of any additional shares of stock actually received will begin on the date that the new ISO is exercised. For purposes of section 422(a)(1), the holding period of all shares, including those shares deemed to be received and those actually received, will begin on the date the new ISO is exercised.

(2) An optionee who constructively pays the exercise price of an ISO with Payment Shares that were previously acquired through the exercise of an ISO but that have not satisfied the holding requirements of Section 422(a) of the Code ("Immature ISO Stock") would receive the same tax treatment as if the optionee had physically surrendered shares that had not satisfied the holding period, specifically:

(a) The constructive surrender of the Payment Shares is a disqualified disposition of those shares that will result in the recognition of compensation income under the rules of section 421(b) and 422(c)(2). See also section 424(c)(3). Any additional appreciation in the value of the stock that is not taxed as compensation income under the disqualified disposition rules is subject to the nonrecognition rules of section 1036.

(b) The basis of the shares deemed to be received that are equal in number to the Payment Shares will be the basis of the Payment Shares increased by any reported compensation income as a result of the disqualified disposition. Any additional shares actually received will have a basis equal to the amount of cash paid, if any, to exercise the new ISO. Sections 424(c)(3) and 1012.

(c) The optionee will not recognize income upon receiving the new shares of stock as a result of the exercise of the ISO. Section 422(c)(4)(A).

(d) For purposes of section 1223(1), the optionee will have a carryover holding period with respect to those shares of stock deemed to be received that are equal in number to the Payment Shares, whereas the holding period of any additional shares of stock received will begin on the date that the new ISO is exercised. For purposes of section 422(a)(1), the holding period of all shares, including those shares deemed to be received and those actually received, will begin on the date the new ISO is exercised.

(3) An optionee who constructively pays the exercise price of an NQSO with Payment Shares that are Mature ISO Stock, Immature ISO Stock, NQSO Stock, or stock that was purchased on the open market would receive the same tax treatment as if the optionee had physically surrendered the shares, specifically:

(a) The optionee will recognize as compensation income the fair market value of the shares that exceed the number Payment Shares used to exercise the NQSO, less cash, if any, paid on the transfer. Section 83 and section 1.83-7 of the regulations;

(b) The optionee will not recognize income upon the constructive exchange of the Payment Shares for those shares of stock received that are equal in number to the Payment

Shares. Section 1036(a), example 4 of section 1.422A-2(i)(4) of the proposed regulations, and Rev. Rul. 80-244;

(c) The optionee will have a carryover basis with respect to those shares of stock received that are equal in number to the Payment Shares and a basis in any additional stock equal to the difference between the fair market value of the shares received pursuant to the NQSO and the exercise price of the NQSO, plus any cash actually paid. Sections 1012 and 1031(d), Rev. Rul. 80-244, Ruling 2; and

(d) The optionee will have a carryover holding period with respect to those shares of stock received that are equal in number to the Payment Shares, whereas the holding period of any additional shares of stock received will begin on the date that the NQSO is exercised. Section 1223(1).

(4) The Company's interpretation of the Plans to permit an optionee to use the certification procedure outlined above to exercise an ISO through constructive surrender of Payment Shares is not a "modification, extension, or renewal" of the ISO. Section 424(h)

(5) Neither the Code nor applicable regulations require the Company to amend the Plans before instituting the certification procedure described above. Section 1.422A-2(b)(1) of the proposed regulations.

This ruling is directed only to the taxpayer who requested it. Section 6110(j)(3) of the Code provides that it may not be used or cited as precedent. No opinion is expressed as to the Federal tax consequences of the above transaction under any other provision of the Code.

Temporary or final regulations pertaining to one or more of the issues addressed in this ruling have not been adopted. Therefore, this ruling will be modified or revoked by adoption of temporary or final regulations to the extent that the regulations are inconsistent with any conclusion in the ruling. However, when the criteria in section 11.05 of Rev. Proc. 96-1, 1996-1 I.R.B. 8, are satisfied, a ruling is not revoked or modified retroactively, except in rare or unusual circumstances.

Sincerely yours,
Charles T. Deliee
Assistant Chief, Branch 4
Office of the Associate Chief Counsel
(Employee Benefits and Exempt Organizations)
Enclosure: Copy for section 6110 purposes

IRS NOTICE 87-49, 1987-2 CB 355

Withholding of Tax Upon Disqualifying Disposition

Section 422A(a)(1) of the Code provides that section 421(a) shall apply with respect to the transfer of a share of stock to an individual pursuant to the exercise of an ISO only if the individual does not dispose of the share within two years from the date of the granting of the option or within one year after the transfer of the share to him. If there is a disqualifying disposition of a share of stock acquired by the exercise of an ISO (i.e., a disposition before the expiration of either holding period described in section 422A(a)(1)), section 1.422A-1(b) of the proposed income tax regulations provides, with certain exceptions, that the effects of the disposition are determined pursuant to section 83 and the regulations thereunder.

Section 83(h) of the Code provides in relevant part that in the case of a transfer of property to which section 83 applies, there shall be allowed as a deduction under section 162, to the person for whom were performed the services in connection with which such property was transferred, an amount equal to the amount included under section 83(a), (b), or (d)(2) in the gross income of the person who performed such services.

Section 1.83-6(a)(2) of the income tax regulations provides that if the service provider is an employee of <Page 357> the person for whom services were performed, the deduction provided by section 83(h) of the Code is allowed only if the employer deducts and withholds upon the amount includible in the employee's gross income in accordance with section 3402. This position conflicts with the rule articulated in Revenue Ruling 71-52, 1971-1 C.B. 278, in which the Service ruled that the disqualifying disposition of stock acquired by the exercise of a qualified stock option described in section 422(b) of the Code did not result in the receipt of wages for Federal employment tax purposes.

The Internal Revenue Service has decided that the allowability of a deduction upon a disqualifying disposition of stock acquired by the exercise of an ISO does not depend on whether a corporation described in section 1.422A-1(b)(1) of the proposed income tax regulations deducts and withholds upon the gross income resulting from the disposition under section 421(b) of the Code. Accordingly, to the extent it is inconsistent with this determination, section 1.422A-1(b)(1) of the proposed regulations will not be adopted as a final regulation.

The Internal Revenue Service is reconsidering Revenue Ruling 71-52. Until the results of such reconsideration are announced, the principles of that revenue ruling will apply to a disqualifying disposition of stock acquired by the exercise of an ISO. Pursuant to section 7805(b) of the Code, any determination that the gross income resulting from such a disqualifying disposition is wages for Federal employment tax purposes will be given prospective effect only.

REV. RUL. 80-244, 1980-2 CB 234 -- IRC SEC. 1036

Sec. 1036 -- Stock for Stock of Same Corporation

26 CFR 1.1036-1: Stock for stock of the same corporation.(Also Sections 83, 421, 422, 425, 1031; 1.83-7, 1.421-8, 1.422- 1, 1.425-1, 1.1031(d)-1.)

HEADNOTE:

Employee stock options; payment with stock.

An explanation is provided of the federal income tax consequences of the acquisition of stock pursuant to the exercise of a nonqualified stock option and payment for the stock with identical shares of the corporation's stock that were previously acquired pursuant to the exercise of a qualified stock option.

Text:

ISSUE

What are the federal income tax consequences of the acquisition of stock pursuant to the exercise of a nonqualified stock option, if payment for the stock is made with shares of the same corporation's stock that were previously acquired pursuant to the exercise of a qualified stock option?

FACTS

A corporation, whose outstanding stock consists of a single class of common stock, has a qualified stock option plan described in section 422 of the Internal Revenue Code and a nonqualified stock option plan. An optionee who exercises an option granted under the nonqualified plan may pay for the shares (1) in cash, (2) with previously acquired shares having a fair market value equal to the option price, or (3) with cash and previously acquired shares having a fair market value less than the option price.

On May 1, 1977, an employee of the corporation exercised a qualified stock option and acquired 1,000 shares of stock for 2x dollars. The fair market value of the stock steadily increased, and on July 1, 1979, when the employee exercised a nonqualified option (which was granted after April 21, 1969, and did not have a readily ascertainable fair market value when granted) for 2,000 shares of stock, the 1,000 shares of stock acquired pursuant to the qualified option had a fair market value of 6x dollars. The employee paid for the 2,000 shares of stock received pursuant to the nonqualified option with the 1,000 shares of identical stock acquired in 1977 when the employee exercised the qualified option. The nonqualified option price for the 2,000 shares of stock was 6x dollars; however, the fair market value was 12x dollars. Thus, the employee exchanged 1,000 shares of stock with a basis of 2x dollars and a fair market value of 6x dollars for 2,000 shares of stock with a fair market value of 12x dollars.

LAW

Section 421(a)(1) of the Code provides that if a share of stock is transferred to an individual in a transfer in respect of which the requirements of section 422(a) are met, no income results when the share is transferred to the individual upon the exercise of the option with respect to that share.

Section 422(a) of the Code provides that section 421(a) applies with respect to the transfer of a share of stock to an individual pursuant to the exercise of a qualified stock option if no disposition of the share is made by the employee within the three-year period beginning on the day after the day of the transfer of the share.

Section 1.421-8(b) of the Income Tax Regulations provides that a disposition of a share of stock, acquired by the exercise of a statutory option, before the expiration of the applicable holding period, makes section 421 of the Code inapplicable to the transfer of the share. The income attributable to the transfer is treated by the individual as income received in the taxable year in which the disposition occurs.

Section 1.421-8(b)(2) of the regulations provides that section 421 of the Code is not made inapplicable by a transfer before the expiration of the applicable holding period if the transfer is not a disposition of stock as defined in section 425(c).

Section 425(c) of the Code provides that the term "disposition" includes a sale, exchange, gift, or a transfer of legal title, but does not include an exchange to which section 1036 applies.

Section 1036(a) of the Code provides that no gain or loss shall be recognized if common stock in a corporation is exchanged solely for common stock in the same corporation, or if preferred stock in a corporation is exchanged solely for preferred stock in the same corporation.

Section 1031(d) of the Code provides that if property is acquired in an exchange described in section 1036(a), the basis shall be the same as that of the property exchanged.

Section 83(a) of the Code provides that, if, in connection with the performance of services, property is transferred to any person other than the person for whom such services are performed, the excess of (1) the fair market value of the property at the first time the rights of the person having the beneficial interest in the property are transferable or are not subject to a substantial risk of forfeiture, whichever occurs earlier, over (2) the amount (if any) paid for the property, is included in the gross income of the person who performed the services.

Section 83(e) of the Code provides that section 83 does not apply to the transfer of an option without a readily ascertainable fair market value. However, under section 1.83-7(a) of the regulations, if such option is exercised, section 83(a) applies to the transfer of property pursuant to the exercise, and the employee realizes compensation upon the transfer at the time and in the amount determined under section 83(a).

HOLDINGS

The exercise of the nonqualified stock option caused the realization of 6x dollars of income under section 83(a) of the Code.

(1) The exchange of 6x dollars in value of common stock (1,000 shares) for 6x dollars in value of common stock (1,000 shares) qualifies for nonrecognition of gain under section 1036 of the Code. Pursuant to section 1031(d), the employee- shareholder's basis in this 1,000 shares of stock received pursuant to the exercise of the

nonqualified option is the same as the employee-shareholder's basis in the 1,000 shares of stock exchanged therefor <Page 236> (2x dollars). Therefore, a disposition within the meaning of section 425(c) did not occur because section 1036 applies to the exchange of the 1,000 shares of stock that were acquired in 1977 pursuant to the exercise of the qualified option, and the employee-shareholder did not receive income pursuant to section 1.421-8(b) of the regulations.

(2) The additional 1,000 shares of common stock received by the employee- shareholder are compensation for services under section 83(a) of the Code. Accordingly, the employee-shareholder must include in gross income the fair market value (6x dollars) of the additional 1,000 shares of stock received pursuant to the exercise of the nonqualified stock option. The employee-shareholder's basis in the additional 1,000 shares of stock is the same as the amount included in gross income (6x dollars).

§ 1.83-2 ELECTION TO INCLUDE IN GROSS INCOME IN YEAR OF TRANSFER

Caution: The Treasury has not yet amended Reg §1.83-2 to reflect changes made by P.L. 99-514, P.L. 98-369.

(a) In general. If property is transferred (within the meaning of § 1.83-3(a)) in connection with the performance of services, the person performing such services may elect to include in gross income under section 83(b) the excess (if any) of the fair market value of the property at the time of transfer (determined without regard to any lapse restriction, as defined in §1.83-3(i)) over the amount (if any) paid for such property, as compensation for services. The fact that the transferee has paid full value for the property transferred, realizing no bargain element in the transaction, does not preclude the use of the election as provided for in this section. If this election is made, the substantial vesting rules of section 83(a) and the regulations thereunder do not apply with respect to such property, and except as otherwise provided in section 83(d)(2) and the regulations thereunder (relating to the cancellation of a nonlapse restriction), any subsequent appreciation in the value of the property is not taxable as compensation to the person who performed the services. Thus, property with respect to which this election is made shall be includible in gross income as of the time of transfer, even though such property is substantially nonvested (as defined in §1.83-3(b)) at the time of transfer, and no compensation will be includible in gross income when such property becomes substantially vested (as defined in § 1.83-3(b)). In computing the gain or loss from the subsequent sale or exchange of such property, its basis shall be the amount paid for the property increased by the amount included in gross income under section 83(b). If property for which a section 83(b) election is in effect is forfeited while substantially nonvested, such forfeiture shall be treated as a sale or exchange upon which there is realized a loss equal to the excess (if any) of—

(1) The amount paid (if any) for such property, over,

(2) The amount realized (if any) upon such forfeiture.

If such property is a capital asset in the hands of the taxpayer, such loss shall be a capital loss. A sale or other disposition of the property that is in substance a forfeiture, or is made in contemplation of a forfeiture, shall be treated as a forfeiture under the two immediately preceding sentences.

(b) Time for making election. Except as provided in the following sentence, the election referred to in paragraph (a) of this section shall be filed not later than 30 days after the date the property was transferred (or, if later, January 29, 1970) and may be filed prior to the date of transfer. Any statement filed before February 15, 1970, which was amended not later than February 16, 1970, in order to make it conform to the requirements of paragraph (e) of this section, shall be deemed a proper election under section 83(b).

(c) Manner of making election. The election referred to in paragraph (a) of this section is made by filing one copy of a written statement with the internal revenue office with whom the person who performed the services files his return. In addition, one copy of such statement shall be submitted with this income tax return for the taxable year in which such property was transferred.

(d) Additional copies. The person who performed the services shall also submit a copy of the statement referred to in paragraph (c) of this section to the person for whom the services are performed. In addition, if the person who performs the services and the transferee of such property are not the same person, the person who performs the services shall submit a copy of such statement to the transferee of the property.

(e) Content of statement. The statement shall be signed by the person making the election and shall indicate that it is being made under section 83(b) of the Code, and shall contain the following information:

(1) The name, address and taxpayer identification number of the taxpayer;

(2)   A description of each property with respect to which the election is being made;

(3)   The date or dates on which the property is transferred and the taxable year (for example, 'calendar year 1970' or 'fiscal year ending May 31, 1970') for which such election was made;

(4)   The nature of the restriction or restrictions to which the property is subject;

(5)   The fair market value at the time of transfer (determined without regard to any lapse restriction, as defined in §1.83-3(i)) of each property with respect to which the election is being made;

(6)   The amount (if any) paid for such property; and

(7)   With respect to elections made after July 21, 1978, a statement to the effect that copies have been furnished to other persons as provided in paragraph (d) of this section.

(f)   Revocability of election. An election under section 83(b) may not be revoked except with the consent of the Commissioner. Consent will be granted only in the case where the transferee is under a mistake of fact as to the underlying transaction and must be requested within 60 days of the date on which the mistake of fact first became known to the person who made the election. In any event, a mistake as to the value, or decline in the value, of the property with respect to which an election under section 83(b) has been made or a failure to perform an act contemplated at the time of transfer of such property does not constitute a mistake of fact.
T.D. 7554, 7/21/78.

§ 1.83-3(j) SALES WHICH MAY GIVE RISE TO SUIT UNDER SECTION 16(b) OF THE SECURITIES EXCHANGE ACT OF 1934

(1) In general. For purposes of section 83 and the regulations thereunder if the sale of property at a profit within six months after the purchase of the property could subject a person to suit under section 16(b) of the Securities Exchange Act of 1934, the person's rights in the property are treated as subject to a substantial risk of forfeiture and as not transferable until the earlier of (i) the expiration of such six-month period, or (ii) the first day on which the sale of such property at a profit will not subject the person to suit under section 16(b) of the Securities Exchange Act of 1934. However, whether an option is 'transferable by the optionee' for purposes of §1.83-7(b)(2)(i) is determined without regard to section 83(c)(3) and this paragraph (j).

(2) Examples. The provisions of this paragraph may be illustrated by the following examples:

Example (1). On January 1, 1983, X corporation sells to P, a beneficial owner of 12% of X corporation stock, in connection with P's performance of services, 100 shares of X corporation stock at $10 per share. At the time of the sale the fair market value of the X corporation stock is $100 per share. P, as a beneficial owner of more 10% of X corporation stock, officer of X, is liable to suit under section 16(b) of the Securities Exchange Act of 1934 for recovery of any profit from any sale and purchase or purchase and sale of X corporation stock within a six-month period, but no other restrictions apply to the stock. Because the section 16(b) restriction is applicable to P, 'P's rights in the 100 shares of stock purchased on January 1, 1983, are treated as subject to a substantial risk of forfeiture and as not transferable through June 29, 1983. P chooses not to make an election under section 83(b) and therefore does not include any amount with respect to the stock purchase in gross income as compensation on the date of purchase. On June 30, 1983, the fair market value of X corporation stock is $250 per share.' P must include $24,000 (100 shares of X corporation stock by P for each share)) in gross income as compensation on June 30, 1983. If, in this example, restrictions other than section 16(b) applied to the stock, such other restrictions (but not section 16(b)) would be taken into account in determining whether the stock is subject to a substantial risk of forfeiture and is nontransferable for periods after June 29, 1983.

Example (2). Assume the same facts as in example (1) except that P is not an insider on or after May 1, 1983, and the section 16(b) restriction does not apply beginning on that date. On May 1, 1983, P must include in gross income as compensation the difference between the fair market value of the stock on that date and the amount paid for the stock.

Example (3). Assume the same facts as in example (1) except that on June 1, 1983, X corporation sells to P an additional 100 shares of X corporation stock at $20 per share. At the time of the sale the fair market value of the X corporation stock is $150 per share. On June 30, 1983, P must include $24,000 in gross income as compensation with respect to the January 1, 1983 purchase. On November 30, 1983, the fair market value of X corporation stock is $200 per share. Accordingly, on that date P must include $18,000 (100 shares of X corporation stock x $180 ($200 fair market value per share less $20 price paid by P for each share)) in gross income as compensation with respect to the June 1, 1983 purchase.

(3) Effective date. This paragraph applies property transferred after December 31, 1981.

§ 1.83-7 TAXATION OF NONQUALIFIED STOCK OPTIONS

(a) In general. If there is granted to an employee or independent contractor (or beneficiary thereof) in connection with the performance of services, an option to which section 421 (relating generally to certain qualified and other options) does not apply, section 83(a) shall apply to such grant if the option has a readily ascertainable fair market value (determined in accordance with paragraph (b) of this section) at the time the option is granted. The person who performed such services realizes compensation upon such grant at the time and in the amount determined under section 83(a). If section 83(a) does not apply to the grant of such an option because the option does not have a readily ascertainable fair market value at the time of grant, sections 83(a) and 83(b) shall apply at the time the option is exercised or otherwise disposed of, even though the fair market value of such option may have become readily ascertainable before such time. If the option is exercised, sections 83(a) and 83(b) apply to the transfer of property pursuant to such exercise, and the employee or independent contractor realizes compensation upon such transfer at the time and in the amount determined under section 83(a) or 83(b). If the option is sold or otherwise disposed of in an arm's length transaction, sections 83(a) and 83(b) apply to the transfer of money or other property received in the same manner as sections 83(a) and 83(b) would have applied to the transfer of property pursuant to an exercise of the option.

(b) Readily ascertainable defined.

(1) Actively traded on an established market. Options have a value at the time they are granted, but that value is ordinarily not readily ascertainable unless the option is actively traded on an established market. If an option is actively traded on an established market, the fair market value of such option is readily ascertainable for purposes of this section by applying the rules of valuation set forth in § 20.2031-2.

(2) Not actively traded on an established market. When an option is not actively traded on an established market, it does not have a readily ascertainable fair market value unless its fair market value can otherwise be measured with reasonable accuracy. For purposes of this section, if an option is not actively traded on an established market, the option does not have a readily ascertainable fair market value when granted unless the taxpayer can show that all of the following conditions exist:

(i) The option is transferable by the optionee;

(ii) The option is exercisable immediately in full by the optionee;

(iii) The option or the property subject to the option is not subject to any restriction or condition (other than a lien or other condition to secure the payment of the purchase price) which has a significant effect upon the fair market value on the option; and

(iv) The fair market value of the option privilege is readily ascertainable in accordance with paragraph (b)(3) of this section.

(3) Option privilege. The option privilege in the case of an option to buy is the opportunity to benefit during the option's exercise period from any increase in the value of property subject to the option during such period, without risking any capital. Similarly, the option privilege in the case of an option to sell is the opportunity to benefit during the exercise period from a decrease in the value of property subject to the option. For example, if at some time during the exercise period of an option to buy, the fair market value of the property subject to the option is greater than the option's exercise price, a profit may be realized by exercising the option and immediately selling the property so acquired for its higher fair market value. Irrespective of whether any such gain may be realized immediately at the time an option is granted, the fair market value of an option to buy includes the value of the right to benefit from any future increase in the value of the property subject to the option (relative to the option exercise price), without risking any capital. Therefore, the fair market value of an option is not merely the difference that may exist at a particular time between the

option's exercise price and the value of the property subject to the option, but also includes the value of the option privilege for the remainder of the exercise period. Accordingly, for purposes of this section, in determining whether the fair market value of an option is readily ascertainable, it is necessary to consider whether the value of the entire option privilege can be measured with reasonable accuracy. In determining whether the value of the option privilege is readily ascertainable, and in determining the amount of such value when such value is readily ascertainable, it is necessary to consider—

(i) Whether the value of the property subject to the option can be ascertained;

(ii) The probability of any ascertainable value of such property increasing or decreasing; and

(iii) The length of the period during which the option can be exercised.

(c) Reporting requirements. [Reserved.]
T.D. 7554, 7/21/78.